THE GREAT TREKS OF THE WORLD

Trekking Patagonia's TORRES DEL PAINE

by
Andrew McCluggage

About the Author

Andrew McCluggage is an outdoor writer and photographer from Northern Ireland. After 20 years as a corporate lawyer, he decided to do something interesting and started writing walking guidebooks.

His first book was '*Walking in the Briançonnais*', covering a beautiful part of the French Alps. Since then, he has written a variety of guidebooks for hiking and trekking.

Other Knife Edge Outdoor Guidebooks written by Andrew include:

- **The Tour du Mont Blanc Handbook**
- **Trekking the Dolomites AV1**
- **The Walker's Haute Route**
- **Trekking Everest Base Camp**
- **Trekking Iceland's Laugavegur Trail**
- **Trekking the West Highland Way**
- **Trekking the Hadrian's Wall Path**
- **Walking Chamonix-Mont Blanc**
- **Trekking the Corsica GR20**
- **Trekking the Cotswold Way**
- **Trekking the Tour des Combins**
- **Trekking the Mallorca GR221**
- **Trekking the Tour of the Écrins**
- **Trekking the Coast to Coast Path**
- **Trekking the Cleveland Way**
- **Trekking the South Downs Way**
- **Walking Brittany**
- **Northern Ireland: the Unmissable Walks**
- **The Mourne Mountains**
- **Big Hikes in the Mourne Mountains**

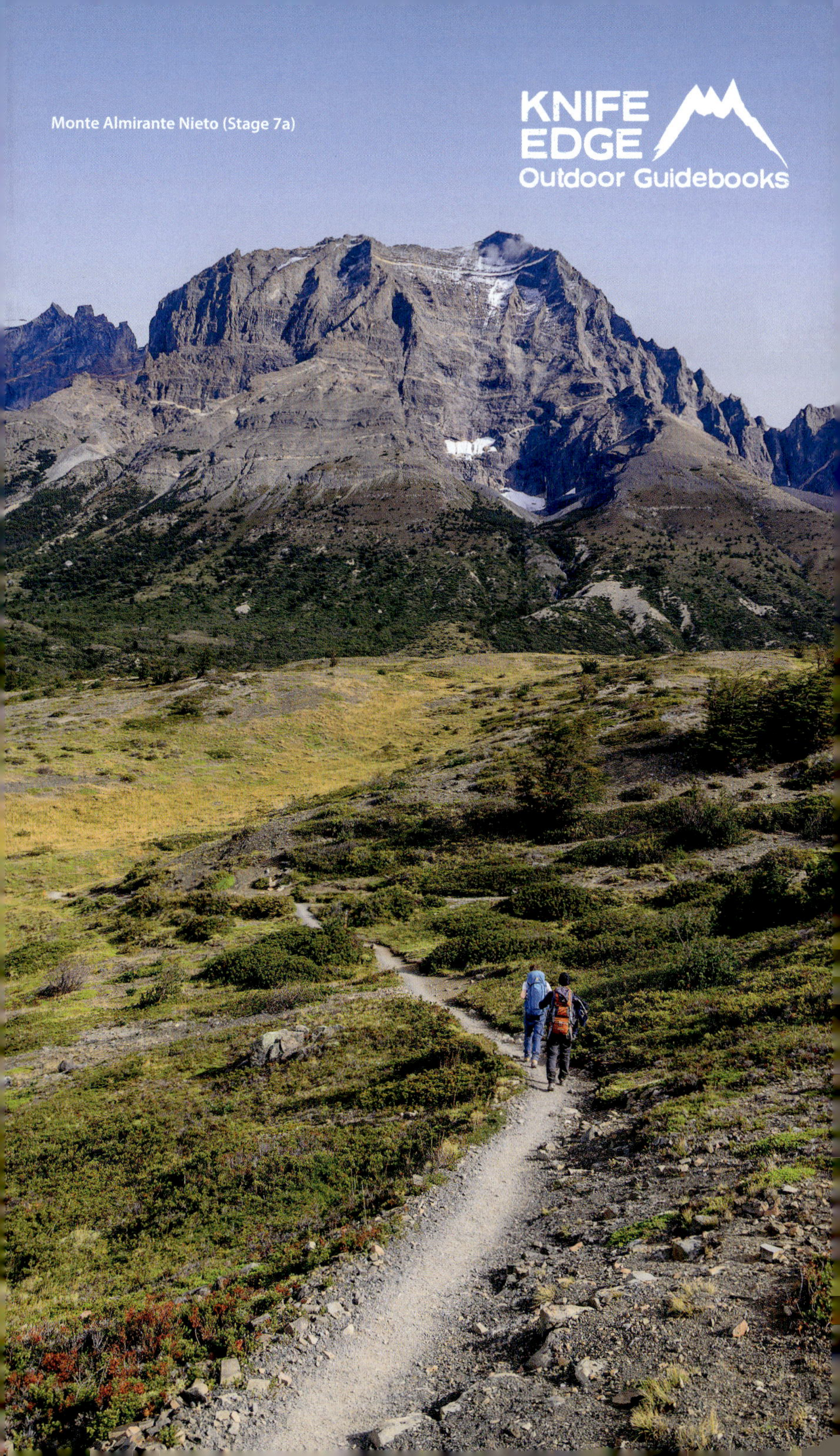

Monte Almirante Nieto (Stage 7a)

KNIFE EDGE
Outdoor Guidebooks

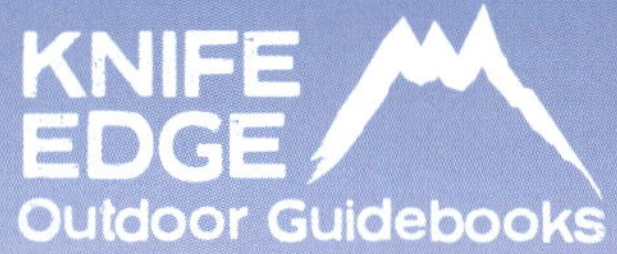

Publisher: Knife Edge Outdoor Limited (NI648568)
12 Torrent Business Centre, Donaghmore, County Tyrone, BT70 3BF, UK
www.knifeedgeoutdoor.com

First edition 2026
ISBN: 978-1-912933-20-4

Map projection: WGS 84 / UTM zone 18S.

A catalogue record for this book is available from the British Library.

Front cover: Sunrise view of the Cuernos del Paine (Mirador Condor)
Back cover: The Towers of Paine (Stage 8a)
Title page: Grey Glacier (Stage 4b)
This page: Monte Almirante Nieto (Stage 8b)

All routes described in this book have been recently walked by the author and both the author and publisher have made all reasonable efforts to ensure that all information is as accurate as possible. However, while a printed book remains constant for the life of an edition, things in the wild often change. Trails are subject to forces outside our control. For example, landslides, avalanches, tree-falls or other matters can result in damage to paths or route changes; waymarks and signposts may fade or be destroyed by wind, snow or the passage of time; or trails may not be maintained by the relevant authorities. If you notice any discrepancies between the information in this guide and the facts on the ground, then please let us know by email (info@knifeedgeoutdoor.com).

Contents

Río Paine valley (Stage 1)

Getting Help

Emergency services number: dial 131 or 133

Distress signal

The signal that you are in distress is 6 blasts on a whistle spaced over a minute, followed by a minute's silence; then repeat. The acknowledgment that your signal has been received is 3 blasts of a whistle over a minute followed by a minute's silence. At night, flashes of a torch can also be used in the same sequences. Always carry a torch and whistle.

Signalling to a helicopter from the ground

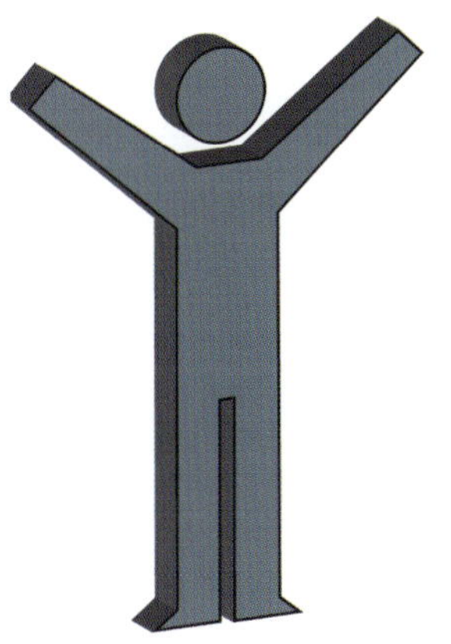

Help Required

Raise both arms in the shape of a 'Y'

Help Not Required

Raise one arm and extend the other arm down and outwards

WARNING

Hills, cliffs and mountains can be dangerous places and walking is a potentially dangerous activity. Some of the routes described in this guide cross potentially hazardous terrain. You walk entirely at your own risk. It is solely your responsibility to ensure that you and all members of your group have adequate experience, fitness and equipment. Neither the author nor the publisher accepts any responsibility or liability whatsoever for death, injury, loss, damage or inconvenience resulting from use of this book, participation in the activity of mountain walking or otherwise.

Some land may be privately owned and we cannot guarantee that there is a legal right of entry to the land. Occasionally, routes change as a result of land disputes.

Cerro Paine Grande at sunrise

The Paso John Garner Tragedy of 2025

On 17 November 2025, just as this book was going to print, five trekkers died in a blizzard on Paso John Garner, the highest point on the O trek. Full details of the tragedy have not yet emerged but it seems that 30-40 hikers, who were approaching the pass from Los Perros, were turned back by heavy snow and extreme winds of up to 190km/h; visibility dropped to only a few metres and wind chill fell to around -20°C. The surviving hikers barely made it back to Los Perros. The brutal weather conditions grounded helicopters and many park rangers had left the park to vote in compulsory elections. Accordingly, it seems that the survivors had to organise rescue attempts themselves. On 18 November, they found bodies near the pass and two of the hikers were still alive; sadly, both died soon afterwards. The following day, weather conditions improved and those with the worst injuries were airlifted to Puerto Natales. The other survivors had to hike out by retracing their steps to the start of the trek.

In the aftermath of the tragedy, the O trek between Central and Grey was closed for many weeks. When it reopened after initial investigations, the park authorities announced a number of new measures designed to reduce risk for trekkers. Firstly, only 100 people will be permitted to cross Paso John Garner each day and registration at Guardería Coirón (Stage 2) will now be compulsory. It is not yet clear how this will operate in practice and we do not know if trekkers will now be prevented from doubling up stages to travel between Serón and Grey (via Paso John Garner) in two days rather than three: however, it is possible that this measure will have some impact on our itinerary planner (p21). Secondly, there will be increased police and ranger presence in the sectors around the pass. In this era of mass tourism, we expect that additional measures will be implemented in the future to regulate trekking in Torres del Paine; although safety will undoubtedly be improved, sadly some of the sense of freedom previously enjoyed in Torres del Paine will be lost.

Introduction

Although every mountain range has its own unique character, the peaks of Torres del Paine National Park (TDPNP) are, without a shadow of doubt, some of the most distinctive in the world. Their unusual shapes, sculpted by glacial erosion, make them tangibly and completely different to any other mountains and there can be few international trekkers who would not recognise TDPNP from a panoramic photograph. The range's character owes a heavy debt to its easy-to-view showpiece, the famous Cuernos del Paine (the Horns) which are so strikingly unusual that they could almost be the setting of a children's fantasy story: when viewed from the south, their otherworldly appearance is hauntingly beautiful and utterly unforgettable, especially at sunrise and sunset. Nevertheless, the national park is named after a better concealed masterpiece, the Torres del Paine (the Towers): three imposing granite pillars, overlooking a surreal turquoise lake, which are the favourites of so many trekkers that their status is practically mythical. Successfully hidden behind the Cuernos, they require more effort to access and are such efficient cloud magnets that those who enjoy clear views of them consider themselves to be pretty lucky.

The Towers and the Horns may be the most talked about peaks in TDPNP but there are legions of other strikingly beautiful mountains too: they are steep-sided, jagged, swathed in vast blankets of the whitest snow, adorned with enormous sparkling glaciers and unattainably high. However, these huge summits do not blend together in anonymity like those in some other mountain ranges because each of these giants is distinctly recognisable and has its own unique character which you will learn to appreciate as the days go by: at 2884m, the glacier-covered Cerro Paine Grande is TDPNP's highest summit and it dominates the W section of the park; in Valle del Francés, you will spot singular beauties such as Aleta de Tiburón (the Shark's Fin), Cerro Espada (an imposing granite spire) and the ramp-shaped Cerro Fortaleza; and adjacent to the Horns, you will find Monte Almirante Nieto (with its huge hanging glacier) which presides over the E part of TDPNP.

However, it is not just the mountains that make TDPNP so special because the park is also filled with spectacular lakes, each having a slightly different colour (which depends upon the quantity and type of rock particles suspended in the water): some, like the wonderful Lago Pehoé are a staggering tint of turquoise (so bright that it is scarcely believable even when viewed with the naked eye); whereas others like Lago Grey are a chilling shade of blue-grey. These broad expanses of water provide a sublime counterpoint to the striking peaks behind and it is no exaggeration to state that the park is a photographer's dream. The vast glaciers of the Southern Ice Field play an important part too, none more so than the vast Glacier Grey which you get very close to in the W of the park.

Whilst these are the tangible attractions of TDPNP, there are also certain intangibles which give it an edge over other destinations. The trail, the accommodation and the scenery all coalesce to imbue the trekker with an intense sense of journey. And that is further amplified by the park's remoteness. TDPNP is only a stone's throw from Antarctica and it feels like the ends of the earth: the nearest town is a few hours away by bus, there are few roads in the park and most of the accommodation is only accessible on foot. It is fair to say that modern development has barely had an impact here and the park is exceptionally well preserved.

Although day-visitors can enjoy many of the highlights of the park, its most remote inner reaches are only accessible on multi-day treks. The original trek is the complete circuit of the park which is known as the 'O' (because on a map the route resembles the letter O): although it is long, if you are seeking more peaceful trails then this is the one to choose. However, the most popular multi-day trek is the 'W' which is basically the S half of the O and takes in many of its highlights: it is easier than the O and unsurprisingly, on a map the route vaguely resembles the letter W. Both of these treks are fabulous choices and are fully described in this book.

With more time, you could add on the wonderful extension that converts the O into the Q (see p120) and we also cover some exceptional day-hikes in other parts of the park which you can undertake before or after your main trek: Mirador Condor, Mirador Cuernos and Mirador Ferrier, for example, provide some of the best panoramic views of the entire TDP massif because they are set further back from it than the routes of the O/W. Because these hikes have road access, they are accessible to day-hikers as well as multi-day trekkers. Whichever hikes you choose, the experience will be unforgettable.

With such amazing sights to experience, it is hardly surprising that these treks are very popular and, in peak season, the accommodation/campsites are full almost every night. Because the W is the most popular trek, its trails are the busiest and this is exacerbated by the fact that the S half of the O uses the same trails as the W; day-hikers can also access the W's trails, adding even more walkers. However, the quantity of people on the trails is rarely oppressive and, if you start early, you can find yourself largely alone for a good part of the day: you will pass, or be passed by, other trekkers but for most people, these fleeting interactions are no bad thing. At night, you will stay in one of the basic, but magnificently situated, refugios/campsites: there you will meet many of the people that you passed earlier in the day, making it easy to develop trail friendships. These are sociable treks and some of the bonds forged can last a lifetime.

The O is approximately 123km long, with 4500m of climbing/descent. The W is 74km long, with approximately 2700m of climbing/descent. These statistics may sound intimidating but it is reassuring to note that thousands of normal people complete the treks each year: with the right preparation, planning and approach, they are manageable for most people of reasonable fitness. Of course, it is a challenge but it is an achievable one. And that is where this book comes in: most of what you need to know to plan, and prepare for, the treks is here within these pages and the entire route is described in detail to guide you on the trail itself. Furthermore, unlike some other books, this one contains real topographical maps: for each stage, there are 1:40,000 scale maps which link with the route descriptions. Because we were unable to find commercially available maps which suited our purposes, we commissioned our own maps and they are perfect for navigating the trail. As well as including those maps in this book, we have also produced a sheet map for TDPNP which is extremely helpful for planning and navigation: '***Trekking Map: Torres del Paine National Park***' (ISBN 9781912933563).

We aim to ensure that you will have the best possible chance of completing your trek. We place great importance on the correct preparation and we focus in detail on the best lightweight gear to carry. We also believe that it is crucial to match your itinerary to your experience, fitness and ability. Accordingly, we have included here an extraordinary level of detail on itinerary planning: our unique itinerary planner has three different multi-day treks (with 18 different multi-day itineraries in total) and a variety of additional day-hikes. For each multi-day itinerary, we have completed for you all the difficult calculations of time, distance and altitude gain/loss. This makes it easy for you to design a manageable itinerary that suits your specific needs. Once on the trail, you will be able to relax and fully enjoy some of the world's great trails.

Patagonia: basic facts

- **Geography:** Patagonia is a distinct geographical region which comprises about 1 million km^2 at the southernmost tip of South America. It spans both Chile and Argentina. Although the exact boundaries of Patagonia are not precisely defined, it is generally accepted that the Pacific and Atlantic oceans form its W and E borders. To the S, the archipelago of Tierra del Fuego is sometimes, but not always, considered to be part of Patagonia. Río Colorado is usually thought to form the northern limit on the Argentinian side, however, in Chile, the N limit is thought to be the town of Puerto Montt (which is further S than Río Colorado). The southern Andes mountain range runs straight through Patagonia, generally along the Chile/Argentina frontier. To the E of the mountains, Argentine Patagonia is a semi-arid region of desert and steppe-like plains, whereas Chilean Patagonia (to the W) is a wet region of mountains, fjords, forests, glaciers and lakes.
- **Name:** the exact origins of Patagonia's name are not known. However, the most popular theory is that it takes its name from the word '*patagón*' which early Spanish explorers used to describe the region's indigenous tribes (which they believed to be a race of giants).
- **Population:** 2 million.
- **Economy:** key industries include agriculture, fishing, mining and tourism.

Torres del Paine National Park

Basic facts

- Located in Southern Patagonia, 112km N of the Chilean town of Puerto Natales, TDPNP is one of South America's crown jewels. It has a unique mix of different ecosystems and comprises about 1,800km^2.
- TDPNP's centrepiece is the exquisite Cordillera del Paine (the Paine massif) which is a spur of the southern Andes and possesses a range of jagged granite peaks which look like nothing else on earth: the massif is surrounded by an indescribably beautiful landscape of awe-inspiring glaciers, otherworldly lakes, formidable rivers and ancient forest.
- The park takes its name from the three tall, thin, peaks known as the Torres de Paine (Towers of Paine). 'Paine' means 'blue' in the native Tehuelche language: the towers are a blueish colour when viewed from a distance.
- The highest mountain in the park is the magnificent Cerro Paine Grande (2884m), however, it is often overshadowed by the more distinctive Horns and Towers.
- The Southern Patagonian Ice Field (the third largest ice mass in the world, after Antarctica and Greenland) forms the W side of TDPNP: it feeds the park's four main glaciers (Dickson, Grey, Zapata, and Tyndall).
- TDPNP attracts more than 250,000 visitors each year.

History

- **Around 8,000 BCE:** the Paine region was first settled by the ancestors of the nomadic Tehuelche people.
- **1558 CE:** Juan Ladrillero, a Spanish navigator and explorer, spotted the Cordillera del Paine from the mouth of the Río Serrano.
- **1879:** Lady Florence Dixie, a Scottish writer, visited the Cordillera del Paine and her group are credited with being its first tourists. When she wrote about her experiences in her book '*Across Patagonia*' (1880), she romantically referred to the three Towers as 'Cleopatra's Needles'. Over subsequent decades, many European scientists and explorers followed in her footsteps. The Chilean government auctioned off land around the massif, enabling wealthy colonialists to create huge estancias (ranches) for cattle and sheep.
- **1959:** the Chilean government created the Parque Nacional de Turismo Lago Grey to protect 5,000 hectares around the Cordillera del Paine.
- **1961:** the surface area of the park was increased to 24,000 hectares.
- **1970:** a further 11,000 hectares were added and the park was given its current name.
- **1976:** John Garner (a British mountaineer) and two park rangers (Pepe Alarcon and Oscar Guineo) marked out the route for a hiking circuit of the Cordillera del Paine, creating what is now known as the O.
- **1977:** Italian count Guide Monzino donated Estancia Río Paine (12,000 hectares) to the Chilean government.
- **1978:** TDPNP was designated a World Biosphere Reserve by UNESCO.

Geology

In simplistic terms, the Paine massif is composed of two different types of rock. It was formed about 12.5 million years ago when granitic magma was forced up through the earth's crust, pushing upwards sedimentary rock (which had formed on the seabed approximately 80 million years previously): eventually, the sedimentary rock was pushed above the surface of the sea. Subsequently, glacial erosion shaped the valleys and peaks by scouring away much of the sedimentary rock and exposing the underlying granite intrusion. The two different types of rock are still easily visible in many of the park's mountains. Most obviously, the Horns have a dark black band of sedimentary rock on their summits, with much lighter coloured granite below: see image on p59.

The incomparable Torres del Paine

Using this book

There are three multi-day treks and numerous day-hikes in TDPNP (with varying levels of difficulty) and in this book, we describe them all. It is important to select a trek/hike which matches your time-frame, experience, fitness and ability. To help you choose between the different options, we have summarised and explained the routes in the '*Torres del Paine's Multi-day Treks*' section of this book (p12): we suggest that you start your planning by reading this part of the book.

Afterwards, our 'Itinerary Planner' (p21) will help you refine your plans. It provides a range of different itineraries for the different treks (18 multi-day itineraries in total). For each itinerary, we have completed for you all the difficult calculations of time, distance and altitude gain/loss. This makes it easy for you to design a manageable itinerary that suits your specific needs.

When you have a rough idea of a suitable itinerary for the trek that you have chosen, you are ready to work out how to arrange the trek and we explain in detail the different ways of doing that (p19). We also explain almost everything else that you will need to know to prepare for the trek.

Finally, once you are on the trek, you can use the route description section of the book (p66) as your guide along the way. As well as fully describing the route, there are detailed maps and elevation profiles to help you know what to expect.

Sections & Stages

This book is designed to be used by walkers of differing abilities. Many guidebooks for long-distance treks rigidly divide the treks into a fixed number of long day-stages, leaving it up to the hiker to break down those stages to design daily routes which suit his/her abilities. This book, however, has been laid out differently to give the trekker flexibility: it divides the treks into shorter stages which you can combine to design daily routes that meet your own specific needs.

We have divided each trek into Sections and Stages and labelled each with a combination of numbers and letters. The labelling is a simple system but requires a little bit of explanation. The first thing to appreciate is that the routes of the treks often overlap and a particular section of path could, in fact, be used by a few different treks/hikes. We have sought to simplify matters by ensuring that each section of path has one label only, even though it is used for multiple treks/hikes. Because the classic TDP circuit (the O) is the original trek in TDPNP, and the other key treks share many of its paths, we have based our labelling system on the stages of the O. Because both of TDPNP's other two multi-day treks (the W and the Q) largely use the same paths as the O, we also use the O's labelling system to describe these treks.

We have divided the O into 8 'Sections', labelled Section 1 to 8 (anti-clockwise from Central): each Section represents one day of our standard itinerary for that trek. Each Section covers the distance between one accommodation option and another subsequent one.

Within some Sections, the route is further broken down into two or more 'Stages': usually, this is because there is a further accommodation option or important junction located mid-Section, and it is useful to understand times/distances for these shorter parts of the route. These Stages are also labelled with a number between 1 and 8, representing the relevant Section that the Stage is part of. Stages are also labelled with a letter: so, for example, the first stage in Section 6 is 'Stage 6a', the second stage is 'Stage 6b' and so on. Take a look at the detailed Itinerary Planner on p21 and all should become clear.

The Itinerary Planner includes a range of tables summarising the multi-day treks and suggesting itineraries for each. For the W (which can be hiked in either direction), we include itineraries for both W-E and E-W trekkers. However, for the O and Q, there are only ACW itineraries because you are only permitted to hike in that direction. In each table, the maths have been done for you so there is no need for you to waste time (and mental strength) working out daily distances, timings and altitude gain/loss.

Of course, the suggested itineraries are only suggestions. You can shorten or lengthen your day to suit yourself: just decide how many Sections/Stages you want to walk that day. It is up to you. As there is accommodation at the end of most Sections/Stages, it is easy to design your own bespoke itinerary. Each Section/Stage has its own walk description and is shown on the route maps.

For example, day 7 of the 8-day O itinerary involves walking Stages 7a and 7b. However, you could decide to extend your day by walking Stages 7a, 7b and 8a, all on the same day. Or you could plan for a short day by walking only Stage 7a. With some other guidebooks, you would have to work out how to split stages yourself, involving some complicated maths to plan distances and times going forward. This guide, however, does all the hard mental work for you.

In this book:

Timings indicate the approximate time required by a reasonably fit walker to complete a stage (excluding stoppage time). Do not get frustrated if your own times do not match ours: everyone walks at different speeds. As you progress through the trek, you will soon learn how your own times compare with those given here and you will adjust your plans accordingly.

Walking distances are given in both miles and kilometres (km). One mile equates to approximately 1.6km.

Place names in brackets in the route descriptions indicate the direction to be followed on signposts. For example, "*('Central')*" would mean that you follow a sign for Central.

Ascent/descent numbers are the aggregate of all the altitude gain or loss (measured in feet and metres) on the uphill or downhill sections of a stage. As a rule of thumb, a fit walker at sea level climbs 1000 to 1300 feet (300 to 400m) in an hour. The ascent/descent numbers for the multi-day treks, set out in the statistics tables in the route descriptions, are based on the O (which is an ACW trek). Accordingly, they also apply unchanged to the W, if hiked W-E: WTs travelling E-W should simply swap the ascent and descent figures.

Elevation profiles are provided for each Section, indicating where the climbs and descents fall on the route. The profiles are based on the O (which is an ACW trek) so they also apply unchanged to the W, if hiked W-E: WTs travelling E-W should simply read the profiles in reverse.

Real maps are provided. These are extracts from 1:40,000 scale maps produced by **Knife Edge Outdoor Guidebooks**. On the maps, we have marked the following: the routes of the treks (**red** for the O; **purple** for the W; **green** for the Q Extension, day-hikes and variants); the start/finish points of stages (yellow markers); significant waypoints (red markers for the O/W; green for the Q Extension, day-hikes and variants); and the accommodation/campsites along the trails. On each map, N is at the top of the page. As well as printing these maps in this book, we have also published a sheet map for TDPNP which is extremely helpful for planning and navigation: '***Trekking Map: Torres del Paine National Park***' (ISBN 9781912933563).

Different colours are used in the text to distinguish different directions of travel. **Blue** is used for information specific to ACW travel (the W travelled W-E and the O/Q); **pink** is used for information specific to CW travel (the W travelled E-W).

The following terms are used:

ACW	Anti-clockwise
BCE/CE	Before the Common Era/the Common Era (secular alternatives to BC/AD)
CW	Clockwise
HLG	Hotel Lago Grey
Horns	The mountains known as the Cuernos del Paine ('Horns of Paine')
LA	Laguna Amarga
O	The O trek
OR	Off-route
OT	O trekker
PG	Paine Grande

PJG	Paso John Garner
PN	Puerto Natales
Q	The Q trek
Q Extension	The additional route which converts the O into the Q (p120)
TDP	Torres del Paine
TDPNP	Torres del Paine National Park
Towers	The three mountains known as the Torres del Paine ('Towers of Paine')
W	The W trek
WT	W trekker

TL	Turn left
TR	Turn right
SH	Straight ahead
N, S, E and W, etc.	North, South, East and West, etc.
N-S/S-N	North to south/South to north
W-E/E-W	West to east/East to west

When to go

Southern Patagonia lies within the world's southern temperate zone and there are four distinct seasons: spring (September to November), summer (December to February), autumn (March to May) and winter (June to August). The trekking season is dictated by climate and normally runs from November to April: outside of this period, some or all of the refugios/campsites may be closed. The peak trekking season is the middle of the period (January/February) and generally, the closer to the fringes of the season, the more unpredictable the weather. However, even in peak season, high winds, heavy rain, and low cloud (which reduces visibility), are common: occasionally, it can even snow on the trail. You might get lucky and hike in fine weather but you should always prepare for the worst. Throughout the trekking season, there is plenty of daylight. The relative merits of each part of the season are discussed in detail below.

November/December: although the weather can be unpredictable, this can be the most beautiful time for trekking. It is often mild during the day (which is perfect for hiking) and the peaks are frequently at their most photogenic, still fully frosted with snow: there is little haze and visibility can be excellent (if the clouds stay away), producing wide-ranging views. However, the wind tends to increase as the period progresses. Furthermore, night temperatures can dip below 0°C so you need to bring plenty of layers. This is peak season for wild-flowers and it is also a good time to spot wildlife (because it is mating season for animals and migratory birds return). Early in this period, there are fewer visitors and accommodation/campsites can therefore be slightly easier to find and significantly, the mountains are more peaceful: however, bookings are hard to come by during the US Thanksgiving holidays at the end of November. Snow sometimes remains on the high parts of the trails, making parts of the route difficult and/or dangerous: in such conditions, crampons/spikes might be helpful. Note that the trails of the more remote N half of the O may open later than the S half (which is shared with the W): this is largely because the winter snow on PJG (the highest point on the treks) takes longer to melt.

January/February: this is the peak summer season when the high parts of the park are normally passable. Days are longest and the chances of good weather are greatest: when the sun comes out, it can be warm. Night temperatures are mild. Although the weather is usually more predictable than in other seasons, the winds can be very strong. Because this is the most popular time for trekking, the park can be very busy and accommodation/campsites are harder to find: advance booking is essential.

March/April: this is our favourite period for hiking. Towards the end of March, visitor numbers thin out and the summer's high winds moderate slightly. Although the weather becomes more unpredictable as the period progresses, skies are frequently clear and daytime temperatures are still mild enough for comfortable hiking. However, evenings get cooler and the days become shorter. April can be a very beautiful time, with spectacular autumn colours. Throughout April, the risk of light snowfall on the high passes increases but any snow usually clears quickly: occasionally, there are more significant dumps of snow in April that adversely impact the safety of trekking for a few days or more. In April, some accommodation/campsites close for the season: the exact date can depend upon the weather.

Period	Pros	Cons
November/ December	Summits still beautifully frosted with snow **Good visibility** Wild-flower season **Good time for wildlife spotting** Fewer trekkers **Accommodation can be easier to find towards the start of the period** Long days	At the start of the period, weather can be unpredictable **Snow can remain on the high parts of the trail, occasionally rendering them inaccessible** Wind starts to increase in November **Cold nights** Thanksgiving period is very busy
January/ February	Most reliable weather **Warm summer sunshine** High parts of the trail normally passable **Long days**	Strong winds **Visitor numbers highest** Accommodation harder to find
March/April	Pleasant daytime temperatures **Good visibility** Fewer visitors **Accommodation becomes easier to find as the period progresses** Autumn colours **Superb sunsets** Slightly less windy than January/February	Towards the end of the period, weather can be unpredictable: increasing possibility of snow **Some accommodation closes towards the end of April** Short days **Cold mornings and nights**

Lago Dickson (Section 2)

Torres del Paine's multi-day treks

To protect the environment, trekking within TDPNP is tightly controlled. Only some of the trails within the park are accessible to tourists: of these, some are freely accessible hiking paths which anyone can use; some are accessible only to hikers on guided tours; and others are set aside for horse riders. All of the treks in this book use the freely accessible paths and you should ensure that you do not stray from them.

There are three multi-day treks in TDPNP and each of them is named after the letter in the alphabet which most closely resembles its shape on a map.

Trek	Direction	Overall Difficulty Level	Days	Total Time (hr:min)	Distance	Ascent	Descent	Max Alt
The O	ACW only	Hard	4-9	42:00	122.9km 76.4miles	4588m 15053ft	4588m 15053ft	1180m 3872ft
The W	W-E	Medium	3-6	25:15	73.9km 45.9miles	2810m 9220ft	2710m 8892ft	900m 2953ft
	E-W	Medium	3-6	25:10	73.9km 45.9miles	2710m 8892ft	2810m 9220ft	900m 2953ft
The Q	ACW only	Hard	5-10	47:30	141.2km 87.8miles	4812m 15788ft	4824m 15827ft	1180m 3872ft

The O: the oldest and classic trek is the complete circuit of the Paine massif. It showcases the massif from every angle and takes in all of its key features including the Towers, the Horns, the Francés valley, Paso John Garner and some exquisite Glacier Grey viewpoints.

The W: although the O is TDPNP's original trek, these days, the W is the most popular one. It is basically the S half of the O and therefore takes less time. It can be considered to be the park's 'greatest hits' trek, taking in most of the main highlights, including the Towers, the Horns and the Francés valley. You can hike this trek W-E or E-W.

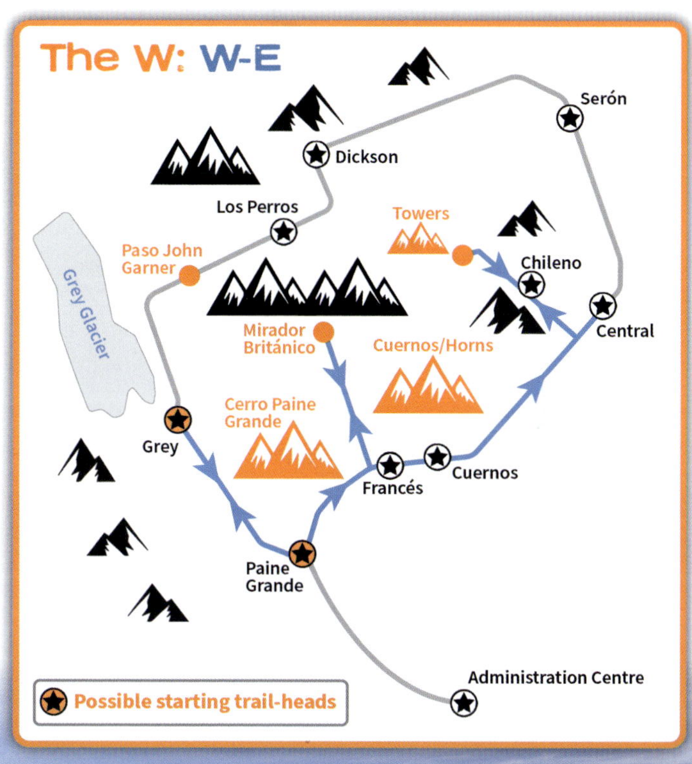

Suspension bridge overlooking Grey Glacier (Stage 4b)

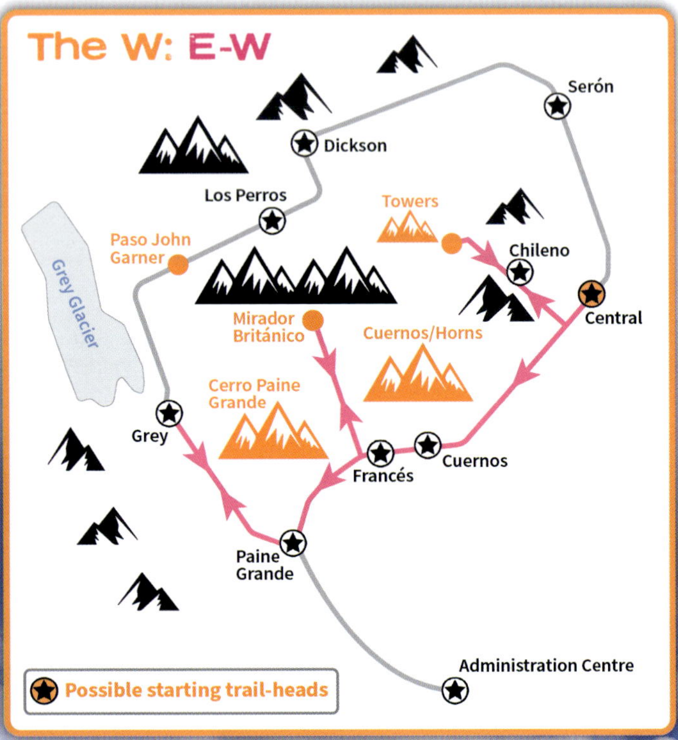

The W: E-W

Serón
Dickson
Los Perros
Towers
Paso John Garner
Chileno
Grey Glacier
Central
Mirador Británico
Cuernos/Horns
Cerro Paine Grande
Grey
Cuernos
Francés
Paine Grande
Administration Centre
Possible starting trail-heads

The Q: this is TDPNP's ultimate trekking experience. The Q is identical to the O except that the wonderful Q Extension is added (see p120).

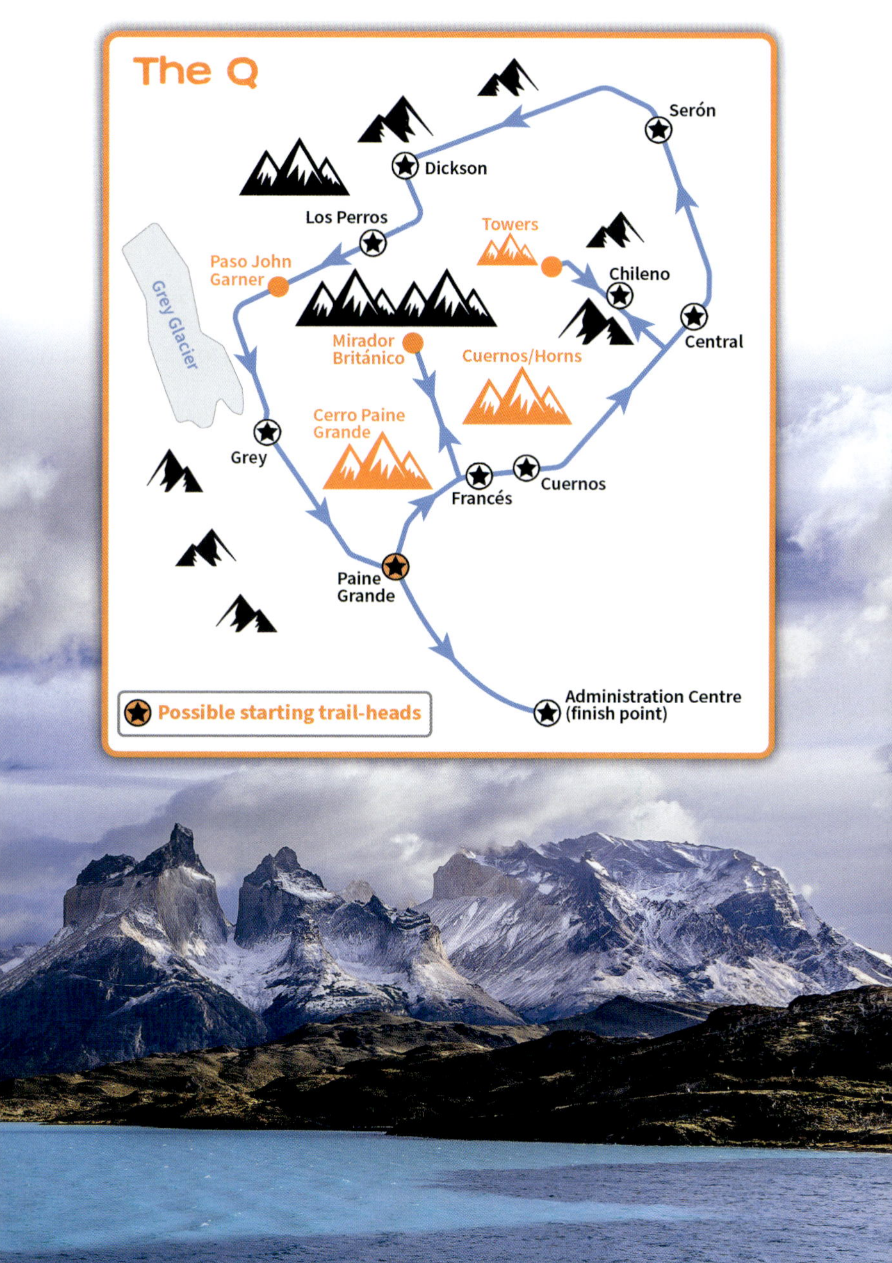

The Torres del Paine massif

Direction

You are only permitted to hike the O and Q in an ACW direction. Furthermore, because you are only allowed to hike the Q Extension N-S (starting at PG), you have to undertake it after completing the O.

However, you can hike the W in either direction: W-E (starting at PG/Grey and finishing at Central) or E-W (starting at Central and finishing at PG/Grey). In our opinion, W-E is preferable because it allows for an easier start to the trek, giving your body a day or two to warm up before the harder stages: if you hike E-W, you start the trek with the tough climb to Mirador TDP (which will be a shock to the system for less experienced trekkers) and some easier terrain is left until last. Otherwise, there is little of significance to split the two approaches.

Trail-heads

There are three starting trail-heads: Central (E side of the massif), Paine Grande (SW) and Refugio Grey (W).

The O: you can start the O at any of the three trail-heads. Because the O is a circuit, you will start and finish at the same place.

The W: you can start the W at any of the three trail-heads. However, because the O is a linear route, you will start and finish at different places.

The Q: you must start the Q at PG and you will finish at the Administration Centre in the far S of TDPNP. You cannot start at the Administration Centre because the Q Extension can only be hiked N-S (starting at PG).

Start/finish trail-head	Pros	Cons	Access (further info on p44)
Central (O/W)	Quickest, easiest and cheapest to access. **Best selection of places to stay and eat.** Shop for basic supplies. **Accessible by car: good parking.**	WTs starting at Central have a tough start to the trek.	Bus from PN to LA + shuttle bus to Central. Alternatively, you can hike from LA to Central (see p116).
Paine Grande (O/W/Q)	One of the largest refugios: plenty of beds and camping pitches. **Good restaurant.** Good shop for supplies. **WTs starting at PG can enjoy an easier start to the W.** Magnificent setting.	Takes longer, and is more expensive, to access than Central. **Not accessible by car.**	Bus from PN to Pudeto (via LA) + boat from Pudeto to PG.
Refugio Grey (O/W)	Good restaurant. **Good shop for supplies.** WTs starting at Grey can enjoy an easier start to the W.	Hardest and most expensive trail-head to access. **Not accessible by car.**	Bus from PN to HLG (via LA & Pudeto) + hike to Lago Grey jetty + boat to Refugio Grey.
Administration Centre (Q: finish only)		Finishing trail-head only. **No shop, restaurant or accommodation.** Buses are infrequent.	Bus to PN (via Pudeto & LA).

How hard are the treks?

The O, W and Q are multi-day treks with significant distances to travel each day. They cross remote landscapes of mountains and valleys: each day, you will need to climb and descend significantly to negotiate the undulating terrain. Sometimes, the climbs/descents are steep and challenging. As the days go by, such exertions take their toll on your body, both physically and mentally. Accordingly, a reasonable level of fitness is required and the fitter you are at the start of the trek, the better your chances of success and the more you will enjoy the experience. Fortunately, altitude acclimatisation is not necessary because hiking elevations within the park are relatively low.

The demand on your body is intensified by the requirement to carry a pack and the burden is greatest for those campers who carry their own tents, sleeping bags, mats and cooking equipment. However, because there are huts (with dormitory beds) and campsites (offering equipped tents) along the route, you do not absolutely need to carry camping equipment or food (other than basic rations) and therefore your pack can be kept light. Even so, it is fair to say that many trekkers set off carrying some equipment which is unnecessary or simply too heavy: this can contribute to injury and/or exhaustion, leading to abandonment. Accordingly, you should give equipment choice careful consideration (see p54): it will be crucial to your enjoyment of the trek and the likelihood of success. Anyone considering carrying camping gear should bear in mind that lugging many kilos of extra gear up the long climbs is hard work.

Paths are largely clear and well maintained although they are sometimes steep, rocky and challenging underfoot. Occasionally, you might have to climb up or down short sections of boulders but you will not require any technical scrambling/climbing skills. Some paths are exposed with large, steep drops.

For the most part, paths/tracks are simple to follow in good conditions. However, occasionally, the route is less obvious and more difficult to navigate: some short sections have no paths at all (for example, across zones of rocks/boulders) and you will have to rely on cairns/waymarks. That said, most people have no major difficulties staying on course. However, take care in poor conditions or low visibility when navigation on the highest sections of the trail can be more tricky. Furthermore, on the high points of the route, snow can remain into late spring/early summer, covering paths and making progress/route-finding more difficult and sometimes dangerous.

However, notwithstanding the challenges, thousands of hikers walk these routes each year. They are therefore achievable endeavours which are within the capabilities of most moderately fit people. However, you will enjoy the experience more if you improve fitness in advance with some training: there is no substitute for training hikes, carrying a pack. Although not absolutely necessary, previous experience of trekking will help. And, of course, the level of difficulty depends upon how quickly, and how far, you travel each day: faster itineraries are obviously more challenging than slower ones and your trek will be more manageable if you select an itinerary that matches your fitness and experience.

By way of comparison, TDPNP's treks have less elevation gain/loss than most Alpine treks of similar lengths. Accordingly, if you have already completed a multi-day route in the Alps then you should find that the O, W and Q are physically easier (provided that you are staying in refugio dormitories or renting equipped tents): however, choosing to carry all your own camping gear will increase the difficulty level somewhat.

The W is the easiest of the three multi-day treks and most people hike it in 4-5 days. However, fit and experienced hikers can finish it in 3 days. Others prefer to walk more slowly, soaking up all the delights on offer. The O is harder than the W, incorporating some wilder terrain (including the crossing of PJG, the most challenging climb in the park). The O's standard itinerary takes 8 days and this suits many trekkers: you can do it faster but the spacing of the accommodation/campsites means that you will have some very long days. The Q is similar in difficulty to the O except that it has one additional long day. Our Itinerary Planner will help you decide what is best for you (see p21).

Hiking shorter sections of the treks

Hiking the O, W or Q in one go is a wonderful experience but there are other ways to enjoy these incredible trails. It is also possible to day-walk parts of the treks using the three main trail-heads as access points (Central, PG and Refugio Grey). If you only want to walk some of the highlights of the treks then the hikes listed below are good options: they are all served by public transport and, in many cases, you can take an early bus into the park and complete a day-hike in time to catch the evening bus back to PN. Alternatively, there is no reason why day-walkers cannot also spend the night at the more accessible huts in the park.

- **Mirador TDP (8b, 8a, 8b; 7.5hr return; p110):** from Central, you can view the famous Towers by hiking to Mirador TDP and back in one long day. All but the fastest trekkers will need to spend a night at Central (before or after the hike). Alternatively, you could overnight at Chileno which is along the route of the hike.
- **Refugio Cuernos (Cuernos-Central Direct Route; 7.5hr return; p118):** from Central, you can hike to Refugio Cuernos and back. Very fit trekkers could complete this in one long day but most people will prefer to split it over two days (spending a night at Cuernos). There are superb views of the Horns and Cerro Paine Grande.
- **Refugio Grey (Section 5; 3.5hr one-way; p90):** take the catamaran from Pudeto to PG, hike from PG to Refugio Grey, catch the boat from Refugio Grey to Hotel Lago Grey and then take the bus from HLG back to PN. Although you can also do this trip in the opposite direction, the boats heading from Refugio Grey to HLG usually visit Grey Glacier and this is a superb way to finish the trip: not all boats heading from HLG to Refugio Grey visit the glacier. You could also incorporate a stay at Refugio Grey or HLG.
- **Mirador Grey (Stage 4b; 3hr return; see map on p82):** take the boat from Hotel Lago Grey to Refugio Grey. From there, you are permitted to hike N along Stage 4b as far as the epic Mirador Grey (near 22): not to be confused with the other place also known as Mirador Grey which is near 24 (see p88). On the way, you will cross two exhilarating suspension bridges. The views of Glacier Grey are incredible. Afterwards, you can return to HLG by boat. Alternatively, spend the night at Refugio Grey and the following morning, hike to PG (Section 5; p90) and then take the catamaran from PG to Pudeto.
- **The Q Extension (5.5hr; p120):** this is a magnificent day-hike in its own right. Take the catamaran from Pudeto to PG, hike to the Administration Centre and then hop on the bus back to PN.

Additional day-hikes

In the S part of TDPNP, there are a number of additional trails which are not part of the W, O or Q. They visit spectacular viewpoints and make great day-hikes: because the viewpoints are set further back from the Cordillera del Paine than the multi-day trails, they offer superb panoramas of the entire massif. Hiking to one or more of these viewpoints is a fabulous way to wrap up your trip to the park. In this book, we describe the following hikes in full and have marked the routes on the maps (in green):

- **Salto Grande/Mirador Cuernos (p124):** Salto Grande is TDPNP's most famous waterfall and Mirador Cuernos is one of the best places to view the Horns. You can access both from Pudeto where the catamaran to/from PG docks: this makes it easy to visit these places before or after your main trek.
- **Mirador Condor (p128):** this viewpoint is one of our favourite places in the park, offering sublime views of the entire Cordillera del Paine and the chance of spotting condors (which nest nearby).
- **Mirador Ferrier (p132):** although this is one of TDPNP's least frequented viewpoints, it is one of the best. There are fabulous views of Glacier Grey, Glacier Pingo and many of the park's huge lakes. The start is located near Hotel Lago Grey: this makes it possible to do the hike before or after your main trek.

- **Isla de los Hielos (p134):** this excellent hike around 'Ice Island' has superb views of Lago Grey and any icebergs which have broken off Glacier Grey. The start is located near the boat jetty for Hotel Lago Grey: this makes it possible to do the hike before or after your main trek.

Guided tours, self-guided tours or independent walking?

Generally, there are two ways to organise a TDP trek: you can either book an organised tour with a trekking company or you can trek independently (not part of an organised tour). The choice is a personal one and depends upon your own particular circumstances and requirements.

Trekking independently

Independent trekkers plan and organise the trek themselves, making any required bookings without the help of a trekking company. They also hike the trail without the support or assistance of a trekking company: the independent trekker is therefore responsible for all daily decisions such as pacing, which way to go at junctions, when to stock up with food/water, and choice of route in bad weather. Navigating a trek independently is extremely satisfying and the sense of achievement on completion is to be savoured: if you have not done it before, it can be almost life-changing, opening the door for other challenges in the future. It offers a greater sense of freedom and adventure and many prefer it to trekking in an organised group. However, for some, trekking independently would be too great a burden on top of the physical effort required simply to walk the route and a guided organised trek can therefore be preferable.

The main advantage of independent trekking is that costs are much lower because you do not have to pay the premium that trekking companies charge for their services. However, the principal disadvantage is that you get no help at all with the difficult process of booking TDP accommodation which is time consuming and complicated (see p35). That said, it is perfectly possible to secure a set of bookings with timely planning, perseverance and a certain amount of luck. If you do not have the spare time and energy that the booking process requires, or you want to maximise your chances, then it may be better to use a trekking company and book an organised tour.

In times gone by, a major advantage of independent trekking was that you had the flexibility to change your plans during the trek to respond to adverse weather, fatigue or other factors. These days, however, campsites/huts/hotels are full to capacity throughout most of the season and the chances of being able to change a whole string of bookings on short notice is slim.

Organised treks

On an organised trek, you usually hike a fixed itinerary which you have selected in advance. A trekking company books all the campsites/accommodation along the route you have chosen, in the correct order, saving you a lot of stress and hassle. Finding availability in TDPNP is their job and most are very good at it: the very best companies are wizards, seemingly conjuring available spaces out of thin air and cleverly re-jigging schedules to make itineraries work. These services can be worth every penny of the fee.

People choose an organised tour for many different reasons. For example, it is a great solution for inexperienced trekkers and those who do not have the time or inclination to make their own arrangements. Others are attracted by the peace of mind that comes with having a trekking company make all the arrangements on their behalf. And those travelling alone frequently prefer the comfort and companionship of a guided organised trek.

In recent years, there has been a rise in the number of businesses offering organised tours. Consequently, some of the accommodation along the TDP may be block-booked in advance by the tour companies. At peak times, this makes it harder for the independent trekker to secure accommodation unless booked well in advance. As a result, many confident trekkers (who would be perfectly capable of walking independently) book an organised trek simply to avail of the accommodation booking service. By booking a tour, much of the hassle of planning the trek is alleviated, albeit at a price.

However, selecting a trekking company can be a daunting prospect because there are many to choose from. By using a well-established and respected company, you can usually be confident that your tour will run smoothly and be of reasonable quality. These days, with a quick internet search, you will find numerous companies offering a variety of itineraries but it can be difficult to be sure that the companies are trustworthy. Common complaints include inexperienced guides, overly fast itineraries and hidden extras. Before choosing, read online reviews, talk to company staff over the phone and thoroughly check the terms and conditions on the company website: you can also seek advice on our TDP Facebook group (see back cover flap).

There are two types of organised treks:

Guided treks: generally, this is the most expensive option. For less experienced hikers and those who would not be confident enough to go it alone, a guided trek is a great solution. You could arrange a private tour for just you and your companion(s) or you could book spaces on a larger group: often those travelling alone prefer the companionship of a larger group. The trekking company typically organises food, accommodation and an experienced guide who looks after you on the trail (making all the trekking decisions and enabling the hiker to concentrate on the hiking). Some tour companies may also be able to organise transfer of luggage (by vehicle or porter) to the more easily accessible huts/campsites/hotels within TDPNP, however, the remoteness of many of the huts/campsites means that baggage transfer is not possible at every location: even guided trekkers carry their own gear for nights at the more remote huts on the O; for further information on baggage transfer, see p52. In fact, the guided trekker does not really have to think about anything except booking international flights and some trekking companies can even do that as well.

Self-guided treks: these offer a sensible middle-ground between independent and guided treks and they have become very popular in recent years. Although they are usually cheaper than guided treks, the tour company still books all the accommodation. However, you will trek without a guide, navigating with the help of this guidebook and/or any instructions provided by the tour company. Normally, breakfast and evening meals will be provided and you can request packed lunches. As with guided tours, self-guided tour companies can sometimes organise transfer of luggage to the more easily accessible huts/hotels. Unlike independent trekkers, you will have someone to contact if something goes wrong with your trip.

Refugio Dickson (Section 2)

Trek Itinerary Planner

Choose your itinerary carefully, making sure that it matches your fitness and experience. What looks easy on paper can be much more difficult in practice. If in doubt, opt for a slower itinerary: the last thing you want is to tire yourself out early in the trek; even one extra day can make a big difference. You will be spending a lot of time, money and effort to get to Patagonia and it therefore makes sense to select an itinerary that is likely to help you to succeed comfortably, rather than an itinerary that has a fair chance of leading you towards failure.

The O

Because you are only permitted to walk the O in an ACW direction, all our Itineraries head in that direction. Furthermore, all our O itineraries start and finish at Central: if you prefer to start at PG then simply start reading the tables at that location: Section 6 will be your first day. If you wish to start at Refugio Grey, then Section 5-S will be your first day. At the moment, there is no way to split the tough Section 4 (incorporating the climb over PJG): this is because there is currently no accommodation/camping mid-section.

After the 2025 tragedy (p2), a new rule was introduced which stated that only 100 people would be allowed to cross PJG each day: at the date of press, it was not yet clear if this would impact the ability to double-up stages.

Stage	Start	Finish	Time hr:m	Distance km	Distance miles	Ascent m	Ascent ft	Descent m	Descent ft	Max Alt m	Max Alt ft
1	Central	Serón	4:30	14.1	8.8	334	1096	304	997	390	1280
2	Serón	Dickson	5:50	18.3	11.4	455	1493	415	1362	361	1184
3	Dickson	Los Perros	3:50	11.9	7.4	473	1552	118	387	580	1903
4a	Los Perros	Paso	4:00	8.5	5.3	682	2238	780	2559	1180	3872
4b	Paso	Grey	2:15	7	4.4	183	600	580	1903	481	1578
5-S	Grey	Paine Grande	3:30	10.8	6.7	319	1047	349	1145	273	896
6a	Paine Grande	Italiano	2:30	7.7	4.8	219	719	99	325	170	558
6b	Italiano	Italiano	4:40	12.8	8.0	615	2018	615	2018	770	2526
6c	Italiano	Francés	0:20	1	0.6	37	121	22	72	180	591
7a	Francés	Cuernos	1:00	3.5	2.2	58	190	148	486	215	705
7b	Cuernos	Chileno	4:15	12.2	7.6	613	2011	288	945	471	1545
8a	Chileno	Chileno	3:45	9.6	6.0	490	1608	490	1608	900	2953
8b	Chileno	Central	1:35	5.5	3.4	110	361	380	1247	471	1545

Valle del Francés (Stage 6b)

Suggested O Itineraries

9 Days: our most relaxed O itinerary allows plenty of time to soak up all the sights on offer. It is a great option for less experienced trekkers or those with plenty of time. Day 4 is tough but there is no way around that. Section 6 (which incorporates the side trip to Mirador Británico) is split over two days: on day 6, you walk from PG to Italiano to Refugio Francés (where you spend the night). The following morning, you backtrack to Italiano, from where you climb to Mirador Británico: at the end of the day, you return to Refugio Francés (where you spend a second night). This itinerary may be too slow for fitter or more experienced trekkers.

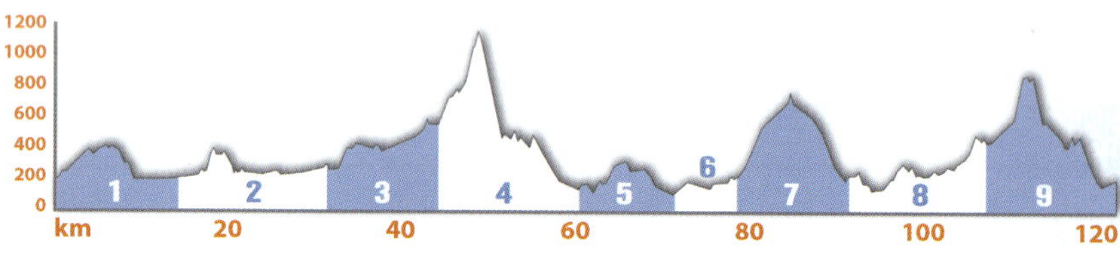

Day	Stages	Start	Finish	Time hr:m	Distance km	Distance miles	Ascent m	Ascent ft	Descent m	Descent ft
1	1	Central	Serón	4:30	14.1	8.8	334	1096	304	997
2	2	Serón	Dickson	5:50	18.3	11.4	455	1493	415	1362
3	3	Dickson	Los Perros	3:50	11.9	7.4	473	1552	118	387
4	4a, 4b	Los Perros	Grey	6:15	15.5	9.6	865	2838	1360	4462
5	5	Grey	Paine Grande	3:30	10.8	6.7	319	1047	349	1145
6	6a, 6c	Paine Grande	Francés	2:50	8.7	5.4	256	840	121	397
7	6c, 6b, 6c	Francés	Francés	5:20	14.8	9.2	674	2211	674	2211
8	7a, 7b	Francés	Chileno	5:15	15.7	9.8	671	2202	436	1431
9	8a, 8b	Chileno	Central	5:20	15.1	9.4	600	1969	870	2854

8 Days: our standard itinerary which is a tried and tested approach. Sensibly balanced days provide an extremely good chance of success. Days 4 and 6 are still quite tough though.

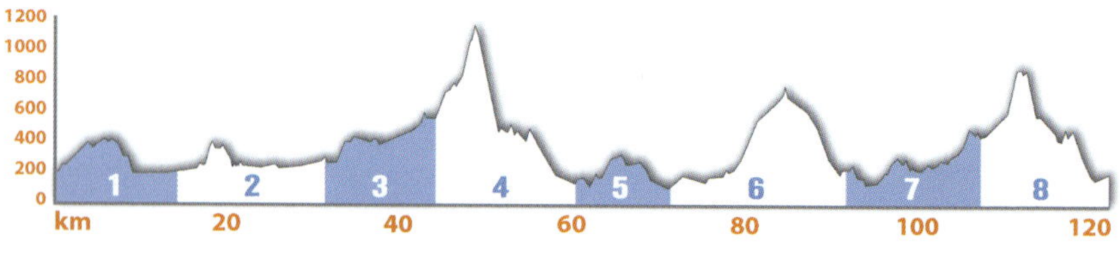

Day	Stages	Start	Finish	Time hr:m	Distance km	Distance miles	Ascent m	Ascent ft	Descent m	Descent ft
1	1	Central	Serón	4:30	14.1	8.8	334	1096	304	997
2	2	Serón	Dickson	5:50	18.3	11.4	455	1493	415	1362
3	3	Dickson	Los Perros	3:50	11.9	7.4	473	1552	118	387
4	4a, 4b	Los Perros	Grey	6:15	15.5	9.6	865	2838	1360	4462
5	5	Grey	Paine Grande	3:30	10.8	6.7	319	1047	349	1145
6	6a, 6b, 6c	Paine Grande	Francés	7:30	21.5	13.4	871	2858	736	2415
7	7a, 7b	Francés	Chileno	5:15	15.7	9.8	671	2202	436	1431
8	8a, 8b	Chileno	Central	5:20	15.1	9.4	600	1969	870	2854

7 Days: similar to the 8-day itinerary except that Sections 2 and 3 (between Serón and Los Perros) are hiked over one very long day. Although this makes for a tough day, it reduces surplus time at Los Perros which is the least comfortable of the campsites: if you hike the short Section 3 on its own, you will have a lot of time to kill there.

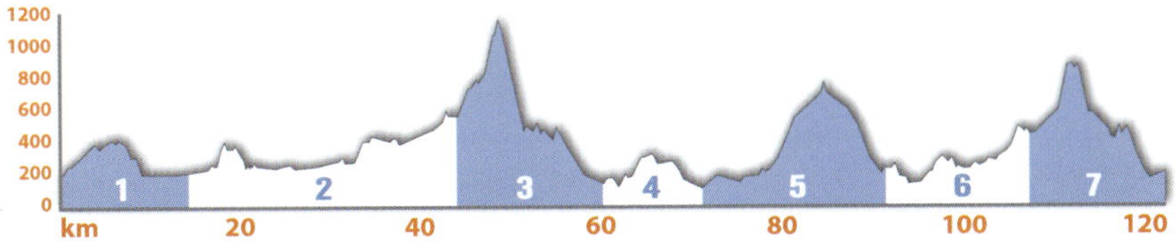

Day	Stages	Start	Finish	Time	Distance		Ascent		Descent	
				hr:m	km	miles	m	ft	m	ft
1	1	Central	Serón	4:30	14.1	8.8	334	1096	304	997
2	2, 3	Serón	Los Perros	9:40	30.2	18.8	928	3045	533	1749
3	4a, 4b	Los Perros	Grey	6:15	15.5	9.6	865	2838	1360	4462
4	5	Grey	Paine Grande	3:30	10.8	6.7	319	1047	349	1145
5	6a, 6b, 6c	Paine Grande	Francés	7:30	21.5	13.4	871	2858	736	2415
6	7a, 7b	Francés	Chileno	5:15	15.7	9.8	671	2202	436	1431
7	8a, 8b	Chileno	Central	5:20	15.1	9.4	600	1969	870	2854

6 Days Option A: similar to the 7-day itinerary except that Sections 4 and 5 (between Los Perros and PG) are hiked over one very long day instead of two: most trekkers will not want to contemplate hiking Section 5 immediately after completing Section 4's tough climb over PJG so this itinerary is for fit and experienced trekkers only. Days 2, 3 and 4 are tough.

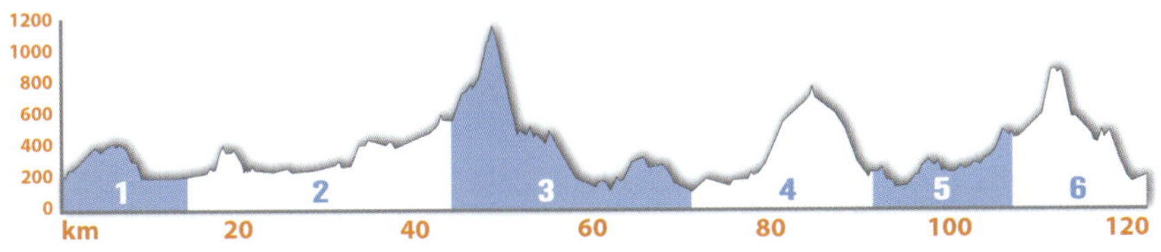

Day	Stages	Start	Finish	Time	Distance		Ascent		Descent	
				hr:m	km	miles	m	ft	m	ft
1	1	Central	Serón	4:30	14.1	8.8	334	1096	304	997
2	2, 3	Serón	Los Perros	9:40	30.2	18.8	928	3045	533	1749
3	4a, 4b, 5	Los Perros	Paine Grande	9:45	26.3	16.3	1184	3885	1709	5607
4	6a, 6b, 6c	Paine Grande	Francés	7:30	21.5	13.4	871	2858	736	2415
5	7a, 7b	Francés	Chileno	5:15	15.7	9.8	671	2202	436	1431
6	8a, 8b	Chileno	Central	5:20	15.1	9.4	600	1969	870	2854

6 Days Option B: for fit and experienced hikers. This is similar to the 7-day itinerary except that Sections 7 and 8 (between Francés and Central) are hiked over one very long day instead of two. Days 2, 5 and 6 are tough. The downside to this approach is that you will be rushing the trip to Mirador TDP on the final day.

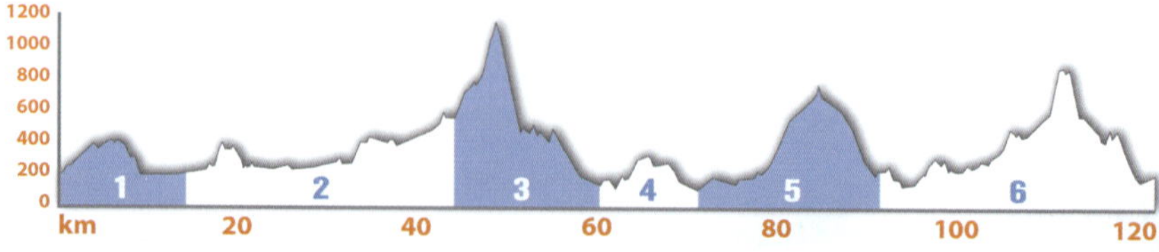

Day	Stages	Start	Finish	Time hr:m	Distance km	Distance miles	Ascent m	Ascent ft	Descent m	Descent ft
1	1	Central	Serón	4:30	14.1	8.8	334	1096	304	997
2	2, 3	Serón	Los Perros	9:40	30.2	18.8	928	3045	533	1749
3	4a, 4b	Los Perros	Grey	6:15	15.5	9.6	865	2838	1360	4462
4	5	Grey	Paine Grande	3:30	10.8	6.7	319	1047	349	1145
5	6a, 6b, 6c	Paine Grande	Francés	7:30	21.5	13.4	871	2858	736	2415
6	7a, 7b, 8a, 8b	Francés	Central	10:35	30.8	19.1	1271	4170	1306	4285

5 Days: a challenging itinerary for very fit and experienced hikers, arriving at the start in very good shape. Sections 2 and 3 (between Serón and Los Perros), Sections 4 and 5 (between Los Perros and PG) and Sections 7 and 8 (between Francés and Central) are each hiked over one very long day instead of two. After a comparatively easy first day, every other day is tough.

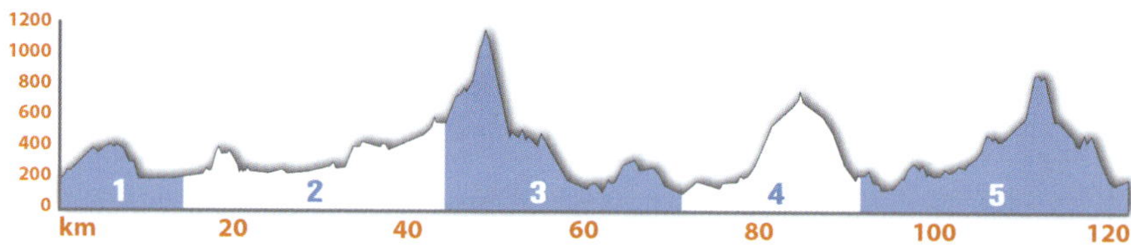

Day	Stages	Start	Finish	Time hr:m	Distance km	Distance miles	Ascent m	Ascent ft	Descent m	Descent ft
1	1	Central	Serón	4:30	14.1	8.8	334	1096	304	997
2	2, 3	Serón	Los Perros	9:40	30.2	18.8	928	3045	533	1749
3	4a, 4b, 5	Los Perros	Paine Grande	9:45	26.3	16.3	1184	3885	1709	5607
4	6a, 6b, 6c	Paine Grande	Francés	7:30	21.5	13.4	871	2858	736	2415
5	7a, 7b, 8a, 8b	Francés	Central	10:35	30.8	19.1	1271	4170	1306	4285

Río Paine (Section 1)

4 Days: an extremely challenging itinerary for fit and experienced trekkers/runners. Every day is long and hard.

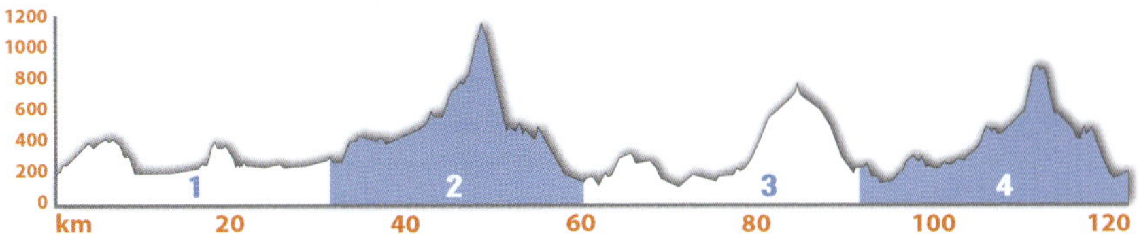

Day	Stages	Start	Finish	Time	Distance		Ascent		Descent	
				hr:m	km	miles	m	ft	m	ft
1	1, 2	Central	Dickson	10:20	32.4	20.1	789	2589	719	2359
2	3, 4a, 4b	Dickson	Grey	10:05	27.4	17.0	1338	4390	1478	4849
3	5, 6a, 6b, 6c	Grey	Francés	11:00	32.3	20.1	1190	3904	1085	3560
4	7a, 7b, 8a, 8b	Francés	Central	10:35	30.8	19.1	1271	4170	1306	4285

Other O options

Our itineraries are not the only possibilities for the O. Here are a few more suggestions:

Valle del Francés: in all our O itineraries (except the 9-day itinerary), Section 6 is completed in full in one long day: you undertake the return hike up Valle del Francés to Mirador Británico on the same day as hiking from PG to Refugio Francés. However, each itinerary can be adjusted slightly by splitting up Section 6 and hiking it over two days: on the first day, walk from PG to Italiano to Refugio Francés and spend the night there; the following day, backtrack 20min to Italiano, climb Valle del Francés and then return to Refugio Francés to spend a second night. For further information see our 9-day itinerary (p22).

Chileno vs Central: in many of our O itineraries, you will overnight at Chileno (which books up very quickly). However, if you cannot secure a booking there, then you can spend that night at Central instead: the following morning, it is possible to climb from Central to Mirador TDP (via Chileno) and back again, all in one very long day: for further information, see p110.

Francés vs Cuernos: Francés is only 3.5km from Cuernos so if you cannot get a booking at the former, you could continue to the latter. Bear in mind though that if you are starting the day at PG and wish to climb to Mirador Británico then this makes for a very long hike: in such circumstances, consider a slower approach by walking this section over two days (see '*Valle del Francés*' above).

A view of the TDP massif (Stage 4b)

The W: W-E

Stage	Start	Finish	Time	Distance		Ascent		Descent		Max Alt	
			hr:m	km	miles	m	ft	m	ft	m	ft
5-N	Paine Grande	Grey	3:40	10.8	6.7	349	1145	319	1047	273	896
5-S	Grey	Paine Grande	3:30	10.8	6.7	319	1047	349	1145	273	896
6a	Paine Grande	Italiano	2:30	7.7	4.8	219	719	99	325	170	558
6b	Italiano	Italiano	4:40	12.8	8.0	615	2018	615	2018	770	2526
6c	Italiano	Francés	0:20	1	0.6	37	121	22	72	180	591
7a	Francés	Cuernos	1:00	3.5	2.2	58	190	148	486	215	705
7b	Cuernos	Chileno	4:15	12.2	7.6	613	2011	288	945	471	1545
8a	Chileno	Chileno	3:45	9.6	6.0	490	1608	490	1608	900	2953
8b	Chileno	Central	1:35	5.5	3.4	110	361	380	1247	471	1545

Suggested W-E Itineraries

All our W-E itineraries start at PG and finish at Central. However, you can also start at Refugio Grey: this avoids the need to walk Section 5 in both directions (saving a half or full day, depending on the itinerary). If you wish to start from Refugio Grey, simply ignore the first stage in the itinerary tables (Stage 5-N) and start the trek with Stage 5-S. Bear in mind though that Refugio Grey is harder to access.

6 Days: our most relaxed itinerary allows plenty of time to soak up all the sights on offer. It is a great option for less experienced trekkers or those with plenty of time. Section 6 (which incorporates the side-trip to Mirador Británico) is split over two days: for more information, see p25. This itinerary may be too slow for fitter or more experienced trekkers.

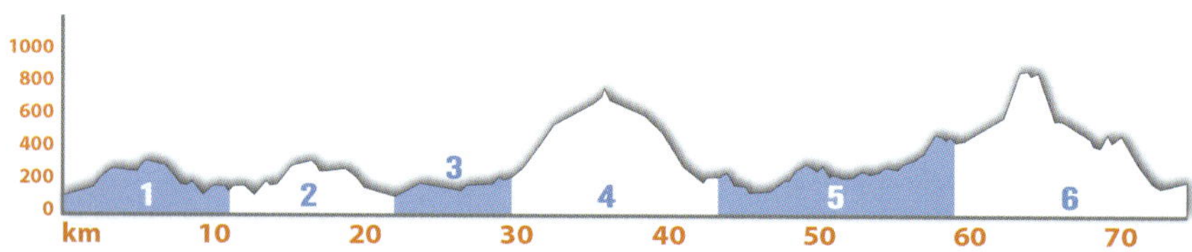

Day	Stages	Start	Finish	Time	Distance		Ascent		Descent	
				hr:m	km	miles	m	ft	m	ft
1	5-N	Paine Grande	Grey	3:40	10.8	6.7	349	1145	319	1047
2	5-S	Grey	Paine Grande	3:30	10.8	6.7	319	1047	349	1145
3	6a, 6c	Paine Grande	Francés	2:50	8.7	5.4	256	840	121	397
4	6c, 6b, 6c	Francés	Francés	5:20	14.8	9.2	674	2211	674	2211
5	7a, 7b	Francés	Chileno	5:15	15.7	9.8	671	2202	436	1431
6	8a, 8b	Chileno	Central	5:20	15.1	9.4	600	1969	870	2854

5 Days Option A: our standard itinerary which is a tried and tested approach. Sensibly balanced days provide an extremely good chance of success. Day 3 is tough but your legs should have warmed up by then.

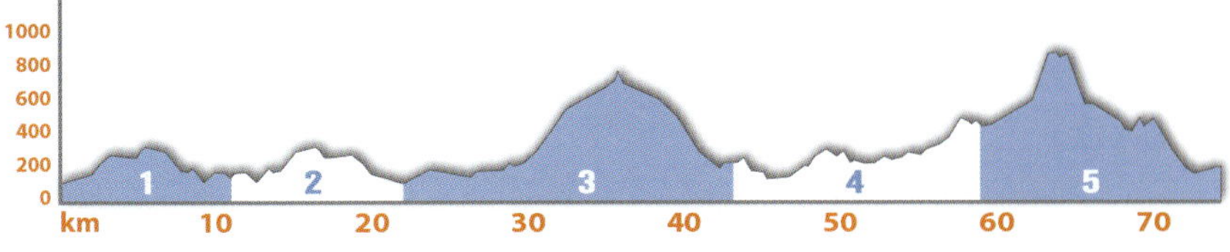

Day	Stages	Start	Finish	Time hr:m	Distance km	Distance miles	Ascent m	Ascent ft	Descent m	Descent ft
1	5-N	Paine Grande	Grey	3:40	10.8	6.7	349	1145	319	1047
2	5-S	Grey	Paine Grande	3:30	10.8	6.7	319	1047	349	1145
3	6a, 6b, 6c	Paine Grande	Francés	7:30	21.5	13.4	871	2858	736	2415
4	7a, 7b	Francés	Chileno	5:15	15.7	9.8	671	2202	436	1431
5	8a, 8b	Chileno	Central	5:20	15.1	9.4	600	1969	870	2854

5 Days Option B: an alternative 5-day itinerary, splitting up the challenging Section 6 (which incorporates the side-trip to Mirador Británico).

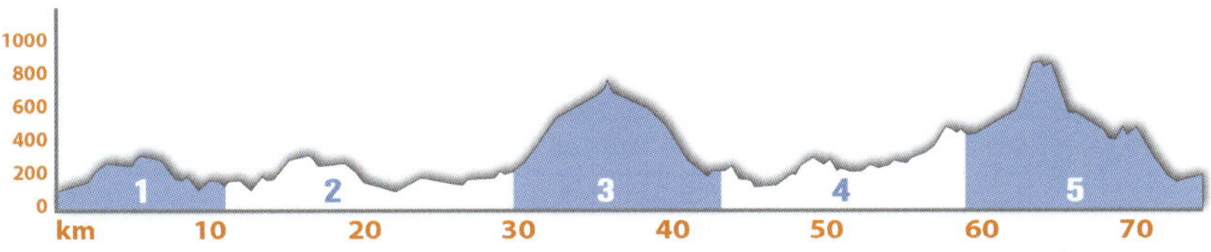

Day	Stages	Start	Finish	Time hr:m	Distance km	Distance miles	Ascent m	Ascent ft	Descent m	Descent ft
1	5-N	Paine Grande	Grey	3:40	10.8	6.7	349	1145	319	1047
2	5-S, 6a, 6c	Grey	Francés	6:20	19.5	12.1	575	1887	470	1542
3	6c, 6b, 6c	Francés	Francés	5:20	14.8	9.2	674	2211	674	2211
4	7a, 7b	Francés	Chileno	5:15	15.7	9.8	671	2202	436	1431
5	8a, 8b	Chileno	Central	5:20	15.1	9.4	600	1969	870	2854

Grey Glacier (Stage 4b)

4 Days: a popular itinerary for those with less time. It is similar to the 5-day Option A itinerary except that the trip from PG to Grey and back is completed all on the first day.

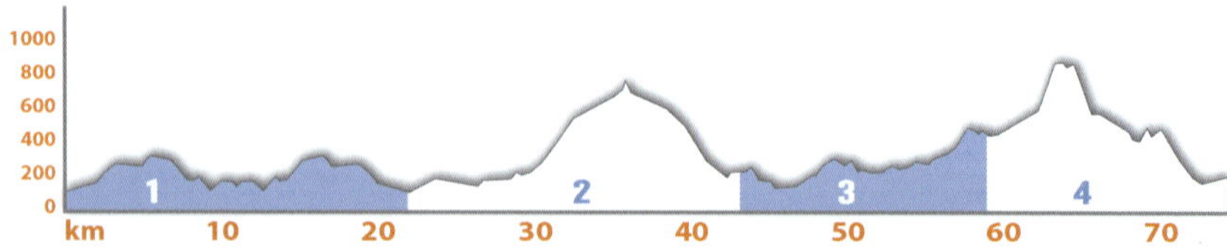

Day	Stages	Start	Finish	Time hr:m	Distance km	Distance miles	Ascent m	Ascent ft	Descent m	Descent ft
1	5-N, 5-S	Paine Grande	Paine Grande	7:10	21.6	13.4	668	2192	668	2192
2	6a, 6b, 6c	Paine Grande	Francés	7:30	21.5	13.4	871	2858	736	2415
3	7a, 7b	Francés	Chileno	5:15	15.7	9.8	671	2202	436	1431
4	8a, 8b	Chileno	Central	5:20	15.1	9.4	600	1969	870	2854

3 Days: a faster itinerary for fit and experienced trekkers/runners. Every day is long and hard.

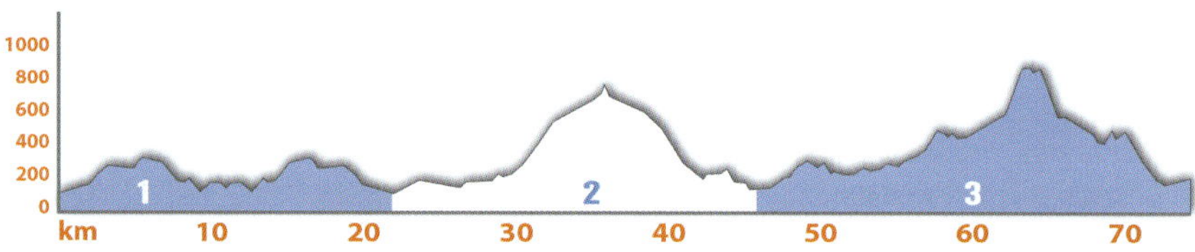

Day	Stages	Start	Finish	Time hr:m	Distance km	Distance miles	Ascent m	Ascent ft	Descent m	Descent ft
1	5-N, 5-S	Paine Grande	Paine Grande	7:10	21.6	13.4	668	2192	668	2192
2	6a, 6b, 6c, 7a	Paine Grande	Cuernos	8:30	25.0	15.5	929	3048	884	2900
3	7b, 8a, 8b	Cuernos	Central	9:35	27.3	17.0	1213	3980	1158	3799

Other W-E options

Our itineraries are not the only W-E possibilities. Here are a few more suggestions:

Valle del Francés: in all our W-E itineraries (except the 5-day Option B and the 6-day itineraries), Section 6 is completed in full in one long day. However, it is also possible to split up Section 6 and hike it over two days: for further information, see p25.

Chileno vs Central: in all our W-E itineraries (except the 3-day itinerary), you will spend your last night at Chileno (which books up very quickly). However, it is also possible to spend that night at Central instead: see p110.

Francés vs Cuernos: Francés is only 3.5km from Cuernos so if you cannot get a booking at the former, you could continue to the latter. For further information, see *"Francés vs Cuernos"* on p25.

The W: E-W

Stage	Start	Finish	Time hr:m	Distance km	Distance miles	Ascent m	Ascent ft	Descent m	Descent ft	Max Alt m	Max Alt ft
8b	Central	Chileno	2:15	5.5	3.4	380	1247	110	361	471	1545
8a	Chileno	Chileno	3:45	9.6	6.0	490	1608	490	1608	900	2953
7b	Chileno	Cuernos	3:35	12.2	7.6	288	945	613	2011	471	1545
7a	Cuernos	Francés	1:10	3.5	2.2	148	486	58	190	215	705
6c	Francés	Italiano	0:20	1	0.6	22	72	37	121	180	591
6b	Italiano	Italiano	4:40	12.8	8.0	615	2018	615	2018	770	2526
6a	Italiano	Paine Grande	2:15	7.7	4.8	99	325	219	719	170	558
5-N	Paine Grande	Grey	3:40	10.8	6.7	349	1145	319	1047	273	896
5-S	Grey	Paine Grande	3:30	10.8	6.7	319	1047	349	1145	273	896

Suggested E-W Itineraries

All our E-W itineraries start at Central and finish at PG. This means that the trek starts with Section 8's tough climb to Mirador TDP (via Chileno): this may be too challenging for some trekkers on the first day. However, if you split the climb over two days, then the first day of the trek is very short (although many trekkers are happy with that because they travel to TDPNP from PN that same day). If you want to hike all of Section 8 on your first day, you will need to catch the first bus from PN.

You can also finish the trek at Refugio Grey instead of PG: this avoids the need to walk Section 5 in both directions (saving a half or full day, depending on the itinerary); if you wish to do this, simply ignore the last stage in the itinerary tables (Stage 5-S) and finish the trek with Stage 5-N. Bear in mind though that Refugio Grey is harder to access.

6 Days Option A: this relaxed itinerary allows for a slower start to the trek. The climb to Mirador TDP is split into two days. Day 1 is very short but this allows plenty of time for travel to TDPNP from PN. However, day 4 (which incorporates the side-trip to Mirador Británico) is pretty tough. This itinerary is a good option for less experienced trekkers or those with plenty of time but may be too slow for fitter hikers.

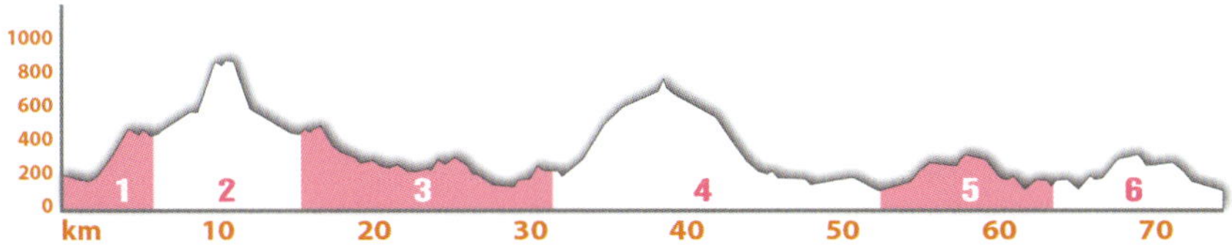

Day	Stages	Start	Finish	Time hr:m	Distance km	Distance miles	Ascent m	Ascent ft	Descent m	Descent ft
1	8b	Central	Chileno	2:15	5.5	3.4	380	1247	110	361
2	8a	Chileno	Chileno	3:45	9.6	6.0	490	1608	490	1608
3	7b, 7a	Chileno	Frances	4:45	15.7	9.8	436	1431	671	2202
4	6c, 6b, 6a	Frances	Paine Grande	7:15	21.5	13.4	736	2415	871	2858
5	5-N	Paine Grande	Grey	3:40	10.8	6.7	349	1145	319	1047
6	5-S	Grey	Paine Grande	3:30	10.8	6.7	319	1047	349	1145

6 Days Option B: in this itinerary, the climb to Mirador TDP is still split into two days. However, days 4 and 5 are restructured: the climb to Mirador Británico is undertaken as a day-hike from Francés (and two nights are spent there); day 5 is slightly longer as Section 5-N (from PG to Grey) is tagged onto the hike from Francés to PG.

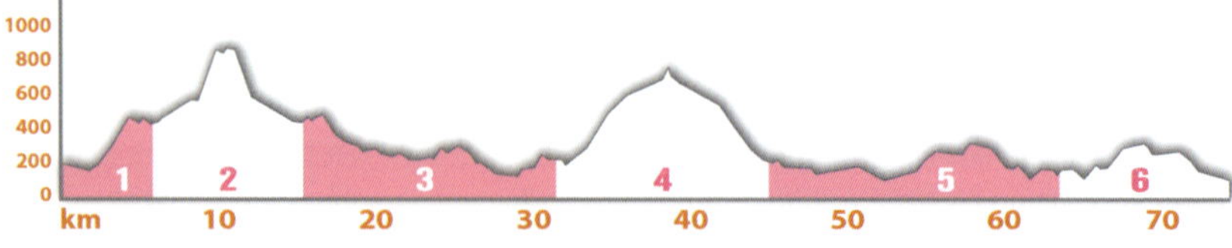

Day	Stages	Start	Finish	Time hr:m	Distance km	miles	Ascent m	ft	Descent m	ft
1	8b	Central	Chileno	2:15	5.5	3.4	380	1247	110	361
2	8a	Chileno	Chileno	3:45	9.6	6.0	490	1608	490	1608
3	7b, 7a	Chileno	Francés	4:45	15.7	9.8	436	1431	671	2202
4	6c, 6b, 6c	Francés	Francés	5:20	14.8	9.2	674	2211	674	2211
5	6c, 6a, 5-N	Francés	Grey	6:15	19.5	12.1	470	1542	575	1887
6	5-S	Grey	Paine Grande	3:30	10.8	6.7	319	1047	349	1145

5 Days Option A: our standard itinerary which is a tried and tested approach. Days 1 and 3 are tough.

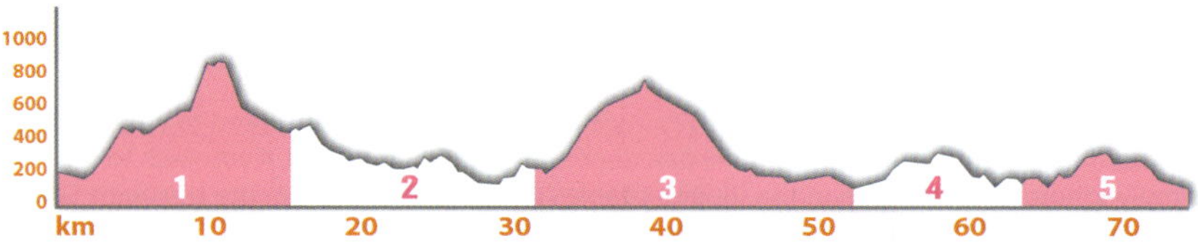

Day	Stages	Start	Finish	Time hr:m	Distance km	miles	Ascent m	ft	Descent m	ft
1	8b, 8a	Central	Chileno	6:00	15.1	9.4	870	2854	600	1969
2	7b, 7a	Chileno	Francés	4:45	15.7	9.8	436	1431	671	2202
3	6c, 6b, 6a	Francés	Paine Grande	7:15	21.5	13.4	736	2415	871	2858
4	5-N	Paine Grande	Grey	3:40	10.8	6.7	349	1145	319	1047
5	5-S	Grey	Paine Grande	3:30	10.8	6.7	319	1047	349	1145

5 Days Option B: an alternative 5-day itinerary that starts with a short first day. The trade-off for this is that days 2, 3 and 4 are all quite challenging.

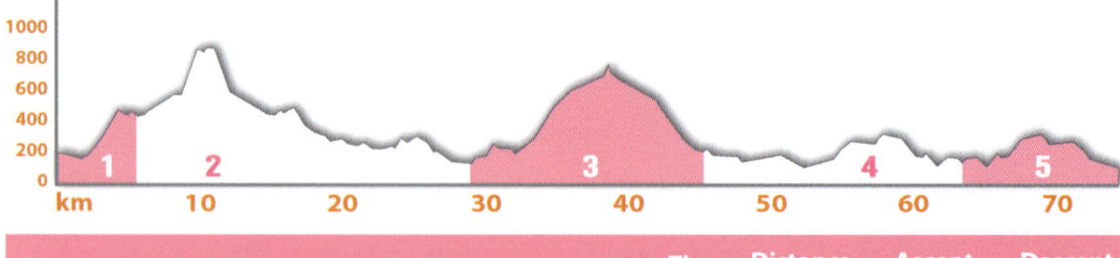

Day	Stages	Start	Finish	Time hr:m	Distance km	miles	Ascent m	ft	Descent m	ft
1	8b	Central	Chileno	2:15	5.5	3.4	380	1247	110	361
2	8a, 7b	Chileno	Cuernos	7:20	21.8	13.5	778	2553	1103	3619
3	7a, 6c, 6b, 6c	Cuernos	Francés	6:30	18.3	11.4	822	2697	732	2402
4	6c, 6a, 5-N	Francés	Grey	6:15	19.5	12.1	470	1542	575	1887
5	5-S	Grey	Paine Grande	3:30	10.8	6.7	319	1047	349	1145

4 Days: a popular itinerary for those with less time. It is similar to the 5-day Option A itinerary except that the trip from PG to Grey and back is completed all on the same day.

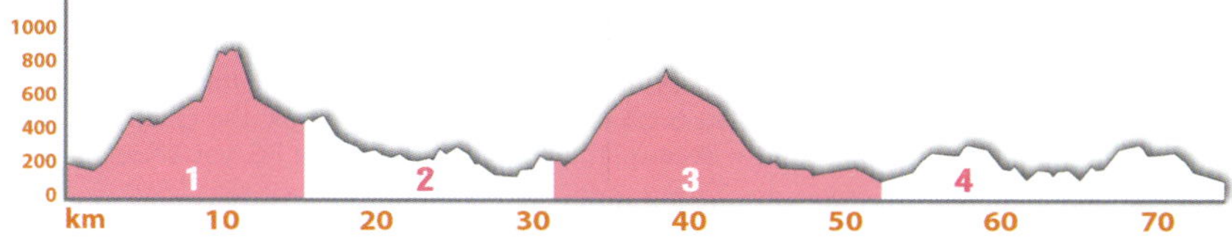

Day	Stages	Start	Finish	Time	Distance		Ascent		Descent	
				hr:m	km	miles	m	ft	m	ft
1	8b, 8a	Central	Chileno	6:00	15.1	9.4	870	2854	600	1969
2	7b, 7a	Chileno	Francés	4:45	15.7	9.8	436	1431	671	2202
3	6c, 6b, 6a	Francés	Paine Grande	7:15	21.5	13.4	736	2415	871	2858
4	5-N, 5-S	Paine Grande	Paine Grande	7:10	21.6	13.4	668	2192	668	2192

3 Days: a faster itinerary for fit and experienced trekkers/runners. Every day is long and hard.

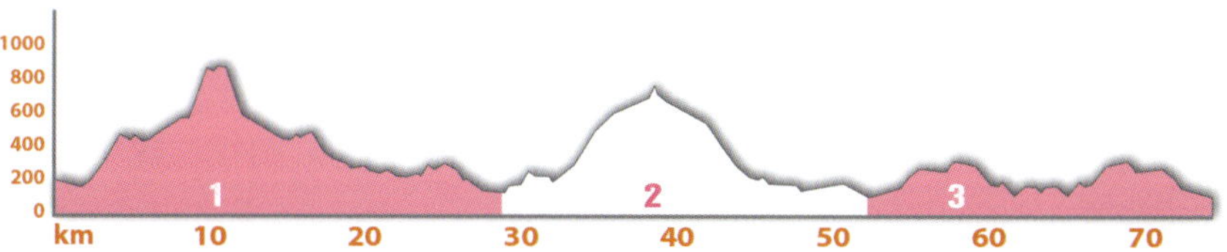

Day	Stages	Start	Finish	Time	Distance		Ascent		Descent	
				hr:m	km	miles	m	ft	m	ft
1	8b, 8a, 7b	Central	Cuernos	9:35	27.3	17.0	1158	3799	1213	3980
2	7a, 6c, 6b, 6a	Cuernos	Paine Grande	8:25	25.0	15.5	884	2900	929	3048
3	5(N), 5(S)	Paine Grande	Paine Grande	7:10	21.6	13.4	668	2192	668	2192

Other E-W options

Laguna Amarga to Central: if you have scheduled a short first day (spending the night at Chileno), consider hiking from the bus stop at LA to Central before starting the W (p116).

Valle del Francés: in all our E-W itineraries (except the 5/6 Days Option B itineraries), Section 6 is completed in full in one long day: you undertake the return hike up Valle del Francés to Mirador Británico on the same day as hiking from Refugio Francés to PG. However, the itineraries can be adjusted slightly by splitting up Section 6 and hiking it over two days: after spending the night at Refugio Francés, walk to Italiano, climb Valle del Francés and then return to Refugio Francés (to spend a second night there); the following day, hike from Refugio Francés to Italiano to PG.

Chileno vs Central: in all our E-W itineraries (except the 3-day itinerary), you will spend your first night at Chileno. However, if you cannot get a booking there, you can spend the first night at Central instead: it is possible to climb from Central to Mirador TDP and back again, all in one very long day. Very fit hikers can even hike from Central to Cuernos (via Mirador TDP) all in one day: for further information, see p110.

Francés vs Cuernos: Cuernos is only 3.5km from Francés so if you cannot get a booking at one, consider staying at the other instead.

The Q

The route of the Q is identical to the O except that the Q Extension is added (see p120). Because you are only permitted to hike the Q Extension N-S (starting at PG), you have to do it after completing the O. Accordingly, all of our O itineraries can be converted into Q itineraries simply by adding the Q Extension as an extra day at the end of the trek: the Q Extension's statistics are set out in the table below. Because the Q Extension starts at PG, you should start and finish the O at PG too.

Additional routes & day-hikes

Route	Start	Finish	Time hr:m	Distance km	Distance miles	Ascent m	Ascent ft	Descent m	Descent ft
Stage 0 (p116)	Laguna Amarga	Central	1:45	5.9	3.7	129	423	79	259
Cuernos-Central Direct Route (p118)	Cuernos	Central	3:50 3:35	12.4	7.7	374	1227	319	1047
The Q Extension (p120)	Paine Grande	Administration	5:30	18.3	11.4	224	735	236	774
Mirador Grey (p88)	Refugio Grey	Refugio Grey	0:25	1.5	0.9	27	89	27	89
Salto Grande (p124)	Pudeto	Pudeto	0:50	2.8	1.7	53	174	53	174
Mirador Cuernos (p124)	Pudeto	Pudeto	2:20	7.8	4.8	140	459	140	459
Mirador Condor (p128)	Hostería Pehoé or Camping Pehoé	Hostería Pehoé or Camping Pehoé	1:00	2.5	1.6	220	722	220	722
Mirador Ferrier (p132)	Rio Pingo Restaurant	Rio Pingo Restaurant	2:50	5.8	3.6	595	1952	595	1952
Isla de los Hielos (p134)	Rio Pingo Restaurant	Rio Pingo Restaurant	1:45	5.6	3.5	98	322	98	322

Río Grey (The Q Extension)

Accommodation

Accommodation in TDPNP

TDPNP's multi-day treks thread their way through mountain terrain, linking huts and campsites which are often difficult or impossible to access by vehicle. Wild camping is prohibited in TDPNP and therefore, before entering the park, trekkers need to arrange a chain of consecutive hut/campsite bookings covering their entire itinerary.

TDPNP is one of the most aspirational trekking locations in the world and demand for accommodation is fierce. Furthermore, because the trek gets more popular each year, finding availability is becoming progressively more difficult and prices are steep. It is no surprise therefore that almost everyone has their entire trip booked before leaving home. In January/February and during the US Thanksgiving holiday (end of November), forward booking is essential: practically every bed/camping pitch along the trail is full every night. December and March used to be shoulder seasons when the trails were much less busy but nowadays, they are only slightly less busy than January/February and advance booking is usually required.

Early November and April are at the fringes of the trekking season and are generally less busy. You may be able to cobble together last minute bookings for this period (especially if you are travelling alone) but do not bet on it: however, we expect this to change in the future as the popularity of TDPNP further increases. In any case, you should exercise caution when arranging a trek at the very fringes of the season: although the weather in April can be divine, it is less reliable and you are more likely to be turned back by snow in high places. Furthermore, if you book the O for early November, you may not know until a few weeks (or even days) before your trek starts whether the winter snow has melted sufficiently to allow for safe hiking: this makes for a stressful run-up to what should be a relaxing experience.

Detailed accommodation listings are provided on p38 and all accommodation is marked on the maps in this book. All contact details were correct at the date of press but this information frequently changes: please let us know about any changes you notice.

Accommodation types

Hotels: there are five hotels within TDPNP but only the luxurious Hotel Las Torres (at Central) lies on the route of the multi-day treks. The other four hotels are slightly OR but it is possible to incorporate them into your itinerary by staying there at the start/end of your trek. EcoCamp Patagonia is located in the E of the park, a short distance from Central. Hostería Pehoé (near the ferry terminal at Pudeto) is the most basic hotel but its location is sublime, looking across the strikingly turquoise Lago Pehoé towards the Horns. The eye-wateringly expensive Explora Torres del Paine is the most luxurious hotel in TDPNP: it is only a few km S of Hostería Pehoé. In the W of the park, you will find Hotel Lago Grey (at the S end of Lago Grey).

Refugios/huts: there are six mountain huts (known as 'refugios') which offer accommodation, meals and drinks (including alcohol). The huts are situated in the heart of the mountains and the settings are spectacular. Some of the huts are only accessible to hikers but a few others can be reached by boat or bus. A stay in a hut can be one of the highlights of a trip to TDPNP, however, in recent years, prices have risen dramatically and they are now extremely expensive: see p47. The huts are run by two different companies: Las Torres operates the huts at Central, Francés and Cuernos; Vertice operates Dickson, Grey and Paine Grande.

At all but one of the huts, the beds are entirely within mixed-sex dormitories (which can take a bit of getting used to if you have not experienced them before). The exception is Refugio Cuernos which has eight private cabins in addition to the dormitory accommodation: you need to book extremely early to snag a cabin. At Las Torres huts, bedding is automatically provided. However, at Vertice huts, you can choose to have sheets and blankets or opt to use your own sleeping bag: the latter option is obviously cheaper.

Refugio Grey

All huts offer hot showers free of charge. Towels are included in the price at Las Torres huts, however, there is an additional charge at Vertice huts. There are facilities for charging electronic devices: sometimes power points are in the bedrooms but otherwise, you may have to queue to use power points in the communal areas. Charging points only operate during the day and are switched off at night.

Campsites: currently, there are nine trail-side campsites. Six of them are located at the park's six mountain huts and share many of the huts' facilities; the other three (Serón, Los Perros and Chileno) are campsites only and have no dormitory facilities. All campsites (except Los Perros) offer prepared meals. All campsites sell drinks and have small grocery shops where you can buy basic food (although the available stock is sometimes very limited). The campsites are run by the same two companies that operate the huts: Las Torres operates the campsites at Central, Serón, Francés, Cuernos and Chileno; Vertice operates Dickson, Los Perros, Grey and Paine Grande. There used to be two additional campsites which were free of charge (Paso and Italiano), however, at the time of writing, these were closed and it is not clear if they will reopen in the future.

At Las Torres campsites, there are three camping packages to choose from (which are progressively more expensive):

- **Basic campsite:** this is simply a bare camping pitch on the ground or a wooden platform. You bring your own tent and camping equipment. This is the cheapest option but it is still very expensive and the requirement to carry all your own gear makes your pack heavier.
- **Semi-equipped campsite:** you rent a tent which has already been erected. Inside the tent, there will be a mattress only: you need to bring your own sleeping bag and camping pillow.
- **Fully-equipped campsite:** you rent a tent, mattress, sleeping bag and pillow. This means that you do not need to carry any camping equipment and your pack will be much lighter. To mitigate the staggeringly high price slightly, this package also includes a welcome drink voucher.

At Las Torres campsites, solo campers pay a hefty single-occupancy premium, making camping an extremely expensive option if you are travelling alone: see p47.

At Vertice campsites, the pricing structure is slightly different. A bare camping pitch is reasonably priced (US$12-14/person) and is very good value for those who are carrying their own equipment. You will pay an additional supplement for each item of equipment you choose to rent (if any): tent, mattress, sleeping bag. At Vertice campsites, there is no premium for single occupancy, however, the price to rent a tent is the same whether you are one or two people (around US$46).

All campsites offer hot showers free of charge, except Los Perros which only has cold water. You will need to bring your own towel. There are power points in the communal areas for charging electronics: you may have to queue. Charging points only operate during the day and are switched off at night.

Camping at Paine Grande

Opening dates

The opening/closing dates for each hut/campsite are different and change from year to year. The huts/campsites on the W usually open from late October to April (weather permitting). However, the more remote huts/campsites on the N parts of the O usually open slightly later in the season and close earlier.

How to book accommodation

Although it is perfectly possible to make accommodation bookings yourself, it requires timely planning, perseverance and a certain amount of luck: if you cannot secure a booking at any one location, then this could render your itinerary impractical or impossible and you may need to cancel bookings already made and start again from scratch (changing dates or adjusting your itinerary). Some people enjoy the process of booking treks but others find it stressful. Plenty of people are successful but others fail because the reservations required have already been snapped up by others. If you do not have sufficient time and energy to give to the booking process, or you want to maximise your chances, then it may be better to use a trekking company (if you can afford it).

Las Torres huts/campsites can be booked online at **www.lastorres.com**: subject to availability, you can book their huts/campsites in whatever order you wish. Vertice huts/campsites can be booked at **www.vertice.travel**: their booking system requires OTs to book all three of Dickson, Los Perros and Grey (in that order); if you wish to hike from Dickson to Grey in one day (without overnighting at Los Perros), for example, you will still have to pay for a night at Los Perros that you do not use (although if you reserve only a bare camping pitch at Los Perros you will only lose US$12). The same applies if you wish to hike from Serón to Los Perros in one day (without overnighting at Dickson). Both Las Torres and Vertice require payment in advance.

Although the original bookings must be made online, currently you cannot cancel or modify bookings online: to cancel or change dates, you need to contact Las Torres or Vertice by email. For Las Torres bookings, if you cancel 90 days or more before the date of your stay, you should receive a full refund; if you cancel less than 90 days before the date of your stay, you will be charged a penalty of 20-80% of the value of your booking. For Vertice bookings, if you cancel more than 60 days before the date of your stay, you should receive a full refund; if you cancel 60 days or less before the date of your stay, you will not receive any refund.

The four TDPNP hotels which are not operated by Las Torres/Vertice (see p39) usually open for booking far in advance. However, the online booking processes for Las Torres and Vertice only begin in April/May for the upcoming season starting in October/November. This does not allow a lot of time to make other arrangements such as booking flights. The process is complicated by the fact that the two companies do not seem to coordinate and open for bookings on different dates. Furthermore, they may not make the exact dates known in advance. If you miss the opening dates even by a few weeks/days, the dates you need could be sold out. This means that it pays to check the two websites regularly and/or contact Las

Torres and Vertice by email to try to find out in advance when bookings will open. The most sought-after dates (January, February and US Thanksgiving) can sell out in a matter of days and you will be competing with trekking companies and a large number of other individuals (many of whom will be checking the websites daily).

Increasing your chances of success

If you do wish to try to book a TDPNP trek yourself then the following steps will help you maximise your chances. The timings recommended below may change because TDP becomes more popular each year.

- **Plan your itinerary before booking opens:** these are complicated treks to book and last-minute planners are less likely to be successful. Finish your research by the end of February for the season starting that November: finalise your proposed itinerary and become familiar with the different accommodation options along the route so that you can make rapid itinerary adjustments if any accommodation you require is unavailable. Reading this book, cover to cover, will help enormously. A spreadsheet is your friend!
- **Familiarise yourself with booking processes:** at the start of March, look at the websites of Las Torres, Vertice and other TDPNP hotels you wish to book. Diarise any booking opening dates listed on the websites and email Las Torres and Vertice to seek updates on booking opening dates. Take a note of the booking method required for each property. You will then be ready to pounce when bookings open.
- **Check websites regularly:** from mid-March onwards, frequently check the websites. Las Torres/Vertice may start taking bookings with little prior notice. By checking regularly, you increase your chances of being one of the first to know that bookings have opened. Some people check websites daily.
- **Pounce:** when any online bookings open, grab your dates immediately. You will need to pay the full price of the booking in advance. Las Torres and Vertice are unlikely to open bookings on the same day and therefore you will probably need to book your trip in two parts. Whichever company opens bookings first, reserve its refuges/campsites immediately and then wait for the other company to open its bookings: hopefully, you will then be able to secure the second portion of your bookings.

Equipped tents at Central

- **Be ready to adapt:** unless you are lucky, you may need to make a few changes to your itinerary before you have a full set of confirmed bookings. The favourable cancellation policies mean that you should receive a refund for any bookings you subsequently need to cancel (see p35). If you have researched the trek well, you will be better placed to make rapid adjustments to your itinerary in the event that any property you want is unavailable on your required date: to avoid having to change already successful bookings, if possible, try to book a different property around the same location as the unavailable property; for example, Francés and Cuernos are interchangeable, as are Chileno and Central. If there is no other available property near the relevant location, try to adjust your itinerary slightly in a way that makes as few changes to confirmed bookings as possible: there is no guarantee that requests for changes to confirmed bookings will be successful. Although it is not optimal, you may need to change the lengths of some of your days, walking a little further than you would like on some days and maybe stopping earlier than you would like on others. However, be careful not to bite off more than you can chew: attempting a hike that is beyond your capabilities can end your trek (or worse). If you do need to change confirmed bookings, the quicker you make the request the better your chance of success.

- **Have a contingency plan (if possible):** even the most persistent and 'sharp-elbowed' people can find themselves at a dead end. If you are beaten, act quickly to implement any contingency plan. For many people, this means contacting a trekking company to book an unguided trek: the quicker you do this, the more likely it is that the company will be able to find accommodation for you. It is a good idea to research trekking companies before bookings open so that you know exactly which one you will go to if you are unable to book the accommodation yourself.

Other booking tips

- Start mid-week. A large number of trekkers start the trail at the weekend. Those who start mid-week are sometimes 'out of sync' with the bulk of the other trekkers and may therefore find accommodation more easily.
- Weekends are often busier: if you can, plan your schedule to avoid hot-spots at weekends.
- Those who hike alone, or in pairs, find it easiest to find beds. For larger groups, it is more difficult.
- Some trekking companies block-book accommodation in advance: even if you cannot find bookings, they might have spaces.
- Occasionally, the last-minute booker can get lucky: people sometimes cancel at the last minute and trekking companies may release unsold beds a few weeks or months before the relevant dates.
- In early November and April, the trails are slightly less busy: however, be aware that the weather can be less favourable in these months.

Accommodation in Puerto Natales

In PN, there is a wide variety of accommodation, catering for all budgets. Before or after your trek, you can choose to stay in a budget hotel/hostel or enjoy one of the town's up-market boutique hotels. In-between, there are numerous comfortable mid-range hotels. Most hotels have their own websites and some have their own booking platforms. Many hotels also sell rooms on generic booking sites such as Expedia.com and Booking.com. The best hotels book up quickly but you can usually find something without booking too far ahead.

Puerto Natales

Accommodation Listings

Trail-side accommodation/campsites

Key on back cover flap.

Stage	Map waypoint	Name	Facilities	Contact details
1/8b Central	1	Central Mountain Hostel	(shop at Welcome Centre)	www.lastorres.com info@lastorres.com +56 22 898 6043 WhatsApp: +56 9 8357 9064
1/8b Central	1	Central Campsite		www.lastorres.com info@lastorres.com +56 22 898 6043 WhatsApp: +56 9 8357 9064
1/8b Central	1	Hotel Las Torres		www.lastorres.com info@lastorres.com +56 22 898 6043 WhatsApp: +56 9 8357 9064
1 Serón	6	Serón Campsite		www.lastorres.com info@lastorres.com +56 22 898 6043 WhatsApp: +56 9 8357 9064
2 Dickson	11	Refugio/ Camping Dickson		www.vertice.travel ventas@vertice.travel +56 22 712 6233
3 Los Perros	16	Camping los Perros		www.vertice.travel ventas@vertice.travel +56 22 712 6233
4a Paso	20	Campamento Paso	Campsite closed at date of press	
4b/5-N Grey	25	Refugio/ Camping Grey		www.vertice.travel ventas@vertice.travel +56 22 712 6233

Stage	Map waypoint	Name	Facilities	Contact details
5- S/6a Paine Grande	31	**Refugio/ Camping Paine Grande**		www.vertice.travel ventas@vertice.travel +56 22 712 6233
6a/6b/6c Italiano	36	**Campamento Italiano**	Campsite closed at date of press	
6c/7a Francés	40	**Refugio/ Camping Francés**		www.lastorres.com info@lastorres.com +56 22 898 6043 WhatsApp: +56 9 8357 9064
7a/7b Cuernos	42	**Refugio/ Camping Cuernos** (see image on p38)		www.lastorres.com info@lastorres.com +56 22 898 6043 WhatsApp: +56 9 8357 9064
7b/8a/8b Chileno	49	**Chileno Campsite**		www.lastorres.com info@lastorres.com +56 22 898 6043 WhatsApp: +56 9 8357 9064

Other TDPNP accommodation

Key on back cover flap.

Location	Map waypoint	Name	Facilities	Contact Details
0.5km from Central	1	**EcoCamp Patagonia**		www.ecocamp.travel
5km S of Pudeto	2	**Hostería Pehoé**		www.hosteriapehoe.cl reservas@hosteriapehoe.cl +56 93 400 5950
7.5km S of Pudeto	3	**Explora Torres del Paine**		www.explora.com reserve@explora.com +1 312 680 3140
6.5km S of Pudeto	4	**Camping Pehoé**		www.campingpehoe.com campingpehoe.fms.cl@ sodexo.com +56 97 499 1958
At the S end of Lago Grey	5	**Hotel Lago Grey**	(shop at nearby Restaurant Río Pingo)	www.lagogrey.com ventas@lagogrey.com +56 61 271 2100

Food

Chile has a huge coastline and vast areas of productive farmland so it is hardly surprising that good meats, fish, seafood, vegetables and fruit are not hard to find in towns like Puerto Natales (where there is a range of restaurants serving local and international food). The fish and seafood, in particular, are often excellent: salmon, mussels, clams and oysters are popular. You will also find many different cuts of steak on menus and you can sample a variety of them if you order an 'asado': this is a mixed grill which is often flame-cooked and usually incorporates a variety of meaty specialties (including choice cuts of steak). The wide variety of fruit and vegetables means that vegetarians and vegans can be reasonably well catered for.

On the trail

Hikers are hungry people and all but one of the huts/campsites/hotels in TDPNP cater for this, providing breakfast, dinner and boxed food (for lunch the following day): the exception is Los Perros where no meals are available and you will need to bring your own food. Generally, the quality of the food provided is pretty good, however, the choices are limited and it is expensive (although that is not surprising when you consider the logistical difficulties in transporting ingredients to these remote locations). If you are relying solely on catered meals, you should book them in advance because numbers are limited and frequently, hikers are turned away. At Las Torres huts/campsites, order meals/boxed lunches online when making your accommodation booking or at least one day in advance by email/WhatsApp. At Vertice huts/campsites, order meals/boxed lunches online when making your accommodation booking or directly at hut/campsite receptions before 15:00 on the relevant day. Vegetarian/vegan options are normally available: request these when you book and remind them when you arrive.

Breakfast: all hotels/huts/campsites (except Los Perros) provide breakfast, if booked in advance. In hotels, there is usually a breakfast buffet with a wide selection of foods: cereals, Chilean bread, fresh fruit, cheese, cold meats, jams, boiled eggs and fresh juices are common. At huts/campsites, the choice is more limited and quality varies: sometimes, there is little more than a continental breakfast of cereal, bread and jam but in others, this may be supplemented with boiled eggs and yoghurt. Coffee and tea are provided but breakfast coffee may be instant/granulated.

Lunch: all of the hotels/huts/campsites (except Los Perros) have restaurants or snack bars where you can order basic snacks, and sometimes larger meals, in the afternoon: the range of food offered can be quite limited; burgers, pizzas and/or sandwiches are typical. The best restaurants are at Central, Dickson, Grey and PG. However, because you may not arrive at your destination until later in the afternoon, and it is often impossible to be sure of what will be available when you arrive, many trekkers prefer to carry boxed lunches (for a picnic along the trail): all hotels/huts/campsites (except Los Perros) can provide boxed lunches, if booked in advance. Typically, a boxed lunch will include a sandwich, a piece of fruit, a chocolate bar and perhaps some nuts. At huts/campsites, it is not generally acceptable to make up a sandwich for lunch using the breakfast food.

Evening meals: all hotels/huts/campsites (except Los Perros) provide evening meals, if booked in advance. Hotels usually have à la carte restaurants. However, at huts/campsites, any à la carte options will only be available during the afternoon and the evening menu will be fixed (so that you have to take what you are offered): usually, there are three courses (starter, main course and dessert). Often, the starter is a vegetable soup. Main courses are often chicken/beef served with vegetables, rice or pasta.

Self-catering: all huts/campsites have covered communal areas (with tables and benches) where you can cook your own food. However, you will need to bring your own camping stove, pot, plate and cutlery which adds weight to your pack. You are not permitted to use stoves outside these areas (because of the risk of bushfire). Furthermore, the use of stoves at Chileno is strictly prohibited so you can only prepare cold food there.

All huts/campsites have small grocery stores where you can buy basic food, however, it is expensive. The items available vary widely and some shops are better than others: at best, you will find candy bars, drinks, dried foods (such as nuts, pasta, rice, lentils) and perhaps some cheese or canned tuna; at worst, you may only find a couple of candy bars. The best shops are at Central, Dickson, Grey and PG; at Serón and Los Perros, there is usually little more than candy bars and crisps/chips. Bear in mind that stocks may run out towards the end of the trekking season.

Basic store at Serón

Because the choice of available food within TDPNP is so limited and prices are high, it makes sense to buy some food in advance in PN before travelling to the park. PN has plenty of shops and supermarkets which sell most of what you need: freeze-dried backpacking meals, however, are harder to find although usually, outdoor stores sell them.

You should choose your food items carefully to ensure that your pack is not too heavy: we cannot emphasise this enough. If you choose food which is too heavy then you may exhaust yourself in the early stages of the trek because your pack will weigh too much. Some people start the trek carrying all of the food they will require for the full distance, however, this may not be a good idea for those not accustomed to carrying heavy packs. It can be preferable to start with only a few days' food, stocking up at shops along the way: it is better to compromise on the quality of what you eat than to exhaust yourself by carrying all your favourite foods. Alternatively, if your budget allows it, you could lighten your load slightly by taking advantage of one or more of the restaurants along the route: perhaps carry your own food for your first few nights and buy prepared meals towards the end of the trek. Make this decision before you start the trek so that you do not carry food that you will not ultimately use.

Water is food's heaviest component and therefore most people carry dried food like pasta or rice. Freeze-dried meals for backpackers are the best choice because they are light and are prepared simply by adding boiling water: you can eat them directly out of the bag so there is no washing-up. These days, there are some very tasty meals available from companies like Real Turmat and Firepot. Canned food is not a good choice as it usually has a high water content and is therefore heavy.

Importing food into Chile

If you are planning to bring food from your home country, you should be aware of the customs restrictions in Chile. Imports of factory-sealed pre-packed food are usually permitted: this means that you can import backpacking meals/snacks containing cooked meat, dairy products, fresh or cooked vegetables and nuts, provided that they are in their original factory packaging. For the avoidance of doubt, jerky is acceptable but raw meat and meat containing bones are not. Pre-packaged fruit is only permitted if it is cooked, candied or preserved. Home-made freeze-dried backpacking meals are not permitted. Remember that regulations change from time to time and you should check them before you travel at **www.sag.gob.cl**.

How much food do I need?

According to the National Health Service (NHS) in the UK, the recommended daily calorie intake is 2,000 calories for women and 2,500 for men. As you will be expending a lot of energy, it seems sensible to increase this slightly: perhaps a minimum of 2,500 calories for women and 3,000 for men. Of course, every person has a different metabolism and will have different requirements but this is a good starting point. Also bear in mind that your daily requirement will depend on how far you are planning to hike each day: the further you hike, the more energy you will use and the more food you will need. Remember also to bring a little extra food (over and above your estimated daily requirements) for emergencies.

Suggested daily menu for self-catering trekkers

Breakfast: instant porridge is a good option because it is light and packed with calories. You can get a variety of different flavours. It is also cheap and, in many countries, it is available in supermarkets. You prepare it simply by adding hot water. You can also buy pre-packed freeze-dried breakfast meals: although they are convenient, they are more expensive.

Lunch & snacks during the day: nuts are hard to beat as they are light and packed with energy. Peanuts, for example, have more calories per gram than most other foods. Dried fruit is also good and will help keep your bodily functions regular. Energy bars and candy can help to provide some variety (and boost moral in tough moments).

Dinner: freeze-dried meals are a good choice. Although they can be expensive, the good quality brands make dinner on the trail something to look forward to. Dried pasta and rice are good too: you can eat these with packet sauces (prepared by adding water).

Central Campsite

Lago Pehoé Catamaran

Travel to Patagonia

TDPNP is located in the S of Chile (at the southernmost tip of South America). Puerto Natales is the closest town to TDPNP (112km S of the park). All trekkers will pass PN both on the way to the park and after leaving it (except for those driving their own car through the Cerro Castillo border crossing; see below). PN has plenty of hotels, restaurants, cafés, bars and shops: accordingly, many trekkers stop there for a night or two to organise their gear and stock up on supplies before travelling to TDPNP. PN also makes a good place to celebrate after your trek.

By air: most trekkers arrive in Patagonia by air on an internal flight from Santiago, the capital of Chile. From Santiago's Arturo Merino Benitez International Airport, there are flights to PN and Punta Arenas (PA), the two closest airports to TDPNP. Because PN is the closest town to the park, it makes most sense to fly directly from Santiago to PN airport (which is only 7km from the town centre). However, the airport is tiny, facilitating a relatively small number of flights each day and tickets between Santiago and PN tend to be expensive. PA is much further away from TDPNP (240km S of PN and 350km S of TDPNP): if you fly there, you will first need to take a bus to PN (3-3.5hrs) before travelling to TDPNP; see p44.

LATAM operates direct flights from Santiago to both PN and PA (**www.latamairlines.com**). Sky Airlines also operates flights from Santiago to PN and PA, however, they are slower because they stop at Puerto Montt (in the Chilean Lake District) before continuing to PN: **www.skyairline.com**. LATAM also operates direct flights between Puerto Montt and PA and Sky operates direct flights from Puerto Montt to both PA and PN.

By bus/car: the vast Parque Nacional Bernado O'Higgins lies immediately to the N of TDPNP and there are no roads through it. Accordingly, the only way to reach TDPNP by road from the N is to travel from Argentina: most people who do this will travel from the Argentinian town of El Calafate (from which you can visit the magnificent Los Glaciares National Park and the Perito Moreno Glacier). Buses travel between El Calafate and PN, crossing the Argentina-Chile border at Río Turbio: Bus-Sur; 5-6hr travel time; contact details on p44. If you have your own car, you can cross more directly between El Calafate and TDPNP (avoiding PN) using the Cerro Castillo border crossing which is further N than Rio Turbio.

By boat: Navimag operates ferries between Puerto Montt and PN which travel through the remote channels of the Patagonian fjords, taking 3-4 days. Although slow, the ferry journey is a unique experience, providing the opportunity to witness some of the world's most remote terrain and spot whales along the way. See **www.navimag.com**.

Travel from Puerto Natales Airport to Puerto Natales

PN Airport is 7km N of the town centre. There are usually plenty of taxis at the airport taxi rank: the journey into town takes around 10min. Some tour companies and upmarket hotels may offer a pre-arranged airport pick-up service.

Travel between Punta Arenas and Puerto Natales

Numerous buses travel each day between PA, PA Airport and PN (3-3.5hr travel time). Current operators include:

- **Bus-Sur:** the region's principal bus operator; book online at **www.bussur.com**; +56 9 9632 3559; sac@bussur.com.
- **Buses Fernández:** book online at **www.busesfernandez.com**.

Travel to the trail-heads

TDPNP has two main gates: Laguna Amarga and Serrano. All buses currently enter and leave the park at Laguna Amarga. If you have your own car, you can enter/leave using either gate. There is a third gate at Sarmiento which is less commonly used and is sometimes closed.

Getting to Laguna Amarga

Many buses travel each day between PN and LA (2hr travel time): this is how most trekkers reach TDPNP. In peak periods, book your return journey well in advance. All buses leave from, and return to, PN's Terminal Rodoviario. Current operators include:

- **Bus-Sur:** 3-4 buses each day between PN and LA. The timetable at date of press is set out on p46. Book online at **www.bussur.com**.
- **Base Torres:** two buses each morning from PN to LA (7am and 9am) and two buses each afternoon from LA to PN (2:15pm and 4:30pm). Book online at **www.basetorres.cl**.

Getting from Laguna Amarga to the trail-heads

Upon arrival at LA, a ranger will board the bus and explain in English and Spanish what you need to do. First, head to a nearby building where your permit will be scanned: sometimes, they also check your accommodation booking confirmations to ensure that you have confirmed accommodation covering the full length of your stay in the park. From LA, your transport choice will depend upon which trail-head you wish to access.

Central: the quickest and easiest trail-head to access. Las Torres runs a shuttle bus from LA to Central (10-15min).

Paine Grande: after registering at the park office, return to the bus that brought you from PN: most buses continue W through the park to the boat jetty at Pudeto (1hr from LA). Buses to/from Pudeto are timed to connect with the catamaran between Pudeto and PG (which takes 30min).

Refugio Grey: the hardest, and most expensive, trail-head to access. Many buses from PN to LA continue W through the park all the way to Hotel Lago Grey (via Pudeto). From HLG, it is 40min on foot to the jetty from which boats run daily to Refugio Grey.

Other places: many of Bus-Sur's buses will stop at other destinations within TDPNP (such as Hostería Pehoé, Camping Pehoé, Hotel Explora and the Administration Centre). For further information, see p45.

Trail-head	Transport from/to Laguna Amarga
Central (O/W)	Las Torres shuttle bus between LA and Central; shuttle buses are timed to connect with the buses from/to PN; $4500 CLP (cash only). Alternatively, you can hike between LA and Central: see p116.
Paine Grande (O/W/Q)	Choose a bus which travels all the way between PN and Pudeto (via LA): Bus-Sur is probably the most popular service. Boats travel between Pudeto and PG (30min travel time); 2-4 boats daily in each direction, depending upon season; $27,000 CLP one way; boats are often full so reserve in advance at **www.catamaranpehoe.com**.
Refugio Grey (O/W)	Choose a bus which travels all the way between PN and HLG (via LA): Bus-Sur is probably the most popular service. Boats travel between HLG's jetty and Refugio Grey: 3 boats daily in each direction; 50% of the boat journeys include a trip to Glacier Grey itself which is a wonderful experience (check in advance); $100,000 CLP one way; reserve in advance at **www.lagogrey.com**. HLG's jetty is 2km on foot from HLG (see p134). Refugio Grey's jetty is 0.6km on foot from Refugio Grey (see p89).
Administration Centre (Q finishing trail-head only)	Bus-Sur travels all the way from the Administration Centre to PN.

Carving of a Magellanic woodpecker

Travelling within TDPNP

Although it is straightforward to travel directly between PN and a specific destination in TDPNP, arranging buses between two destinations within the park can be more challenging. Bus-Sur operates shuttles between Laguna Amarga and Hotel Lago Grey, stopping at Pudeto (where boats leave for PG), Camping Pehoé and the Administration Centre: on request, they will also stop at Hostería Pehoé or Hotel Explora. However, there are only two of these shuttles each day in either direction: if you miss it, you could be in for a very long wait or even find yourself stranded for the night. Bus-Sur also operates a third shuttle from LA which only goes as far as Camping Pehoé. Given the infrequency of the shuttles, it is important to reserve in advance by emailing Bus-Sur (see p44).

Bus-Sur Timetable

(subject to change)

Puerto Natales		Laguna Amarga		Pudeto		Hostería Pehoé (on request)		Camping Pehoé		Administration Centre		Hotel Lago Grey
		Shuttle bus to/from Central		Catamaran to/from Paine Grande								Boat to/from Refugio Grey
07:00	→	09:00	→	10:00	→	10:10	→	10:15	→	11:00	→	11:30
12:00	→	14:00	→	15:00	→	15:25	→	15:30	→	16:00	→	16:30
14:30	→	16:30	→	17:15	→	17:25	→	17:30				
18:00	→	19:30										
13:00	←	11:00	←	10:30								
17:05	←	15:00	←	14:30	←	14:20	←	14:15	←	14:00	←	13:30
21:30	←	20:15	←	19:30	←	18:20	←	18:15	←	18:00	←	17:30

On the Trail

Windy Pass (Stage 7b/8b)

Costs

In tourist areas of Chilean Patagonia, costs are generally comparable with those in Europe or North America. However, TDPNP's status as a bucket list destination means that, within the park, prices are more expensive and in some cases, the costs charged can be outrageous. Unfortunately, as a captive audience, you have little choice other than to accept the pricing, if you want to witness what is certainly one of the most strikingly beautiful places in the world.

In PN, dormitory beds in hostels cost around US$20-25/night. The cheapest double/twin rooms start at around US$40/night (for two people sharing, excluding breakfast): at the other end of the scale, the most luxurious hotel rooms can cost up to US$1500/night. The sweet spot in PN is perhaps around US$100-150/night, for which you should get a lovely room in a central location, including breakfast.

In TDPNP, accommodation prices have exploded in recent years. Even the cost of a lowly camping pitch can make you weep: while Vertice's bare camping pitches are still reasonably priced, the charges at Las Torres campsites are brutal especially if you are travelling alone (solo hikers pay a hefty single supplement). Dormitory beds are also painfully expensive and hotels within the park (except perhaps Hostería Pehoé) are now beyond the means of most people. For a 4-night W hike, expect to spend a total of US$600-800 per person on dormitory beds; campers can expect to spend US$130-230 per person in total on bare campsites (excluding any gear rental) or US$500-740 per person for fully-equipped campsites (with all camping gear supplied).

As regards food, meals in PN are moderately priced, perhaps comparable to those in Europe and North America. However, prices rise dramatically inside TDPNP: unless you are cooking for yourself, you will need to budget for US$110-150/day per person on food. By carrying your own food, you can save a lot of money.

When you add all of this up, the conclusion is quite shocking. For a 4-night W hike, expect to spend a grand total of US$1100-1300 per person on purchased meals and accommodation (if you are staying in dormitories); US$650-1250 per person if you are camping and purchasing catered meals.

	Approximate cost (PN)	Approximate cost (TDPNP)
Dormitory bed in hostel/hut (per person, per night)	US$20-25	US$45-210
Hotel (double/twin room per night)	US$40-1500	US$370-2000
Bare camping pitch (per person, per night)	N/A	US$12-90
Semi-equipped camping pitch (per person, per night)	N/A	US$46-200
Fully-equipped camping pitch (per person, per night)	N/A	US$77-270
Evening meal	US$15-40	US$50-70
Boxed lunch	N/A	US$32-42
Breakfast	US$10-15	US$30-40
Beer (0.5L)	US$5-7	US$5-7
Coke	US$3-4	US$4
WiFi (1 hour)	Free	US$8

Weather

The weather conditions in TDPNP are notorious. Although there is plenty of good weather during the trekking season (November to April), bad weather can appear at any time and, when it arrives, it can be brutal: torrential rain, ferocious wind (for which TDPNP is infamous), thick low cloud (which reduces visibility) and sometimes snow. Furthermore, the weather is notoriously difficult to predict and can change with alarming speed: it is not unusual to experience three or four seasons in a single day. Sadly, recent history shows that weather shifts in TDP can even prove to be deadly: in November 2025, five OTs died in a blizzard, attempting to cross PJG: conditions apparently changed extremely rapidly, with hurricane strength winds arriving with the snow; for further information, see p2.

The main cause of this extreme and capricious weather is TDP's proximity to four major geographical features which have a significant impact on the region's climate: Antarctica (the world's largest ice field), the Pacific Ocean (the world's largest ocean), the Andes (the world's longest mountain range) and the Southern Patagonian Ice Field (the world's third largest ice field). Vicious westerly winds from Antarctica (known as the Roaring 40s and Furious 50s) race across the Pacific Ocean towards Patagonia: in the absence of any significant landmass on the way to slow them down, the winds hit the Andes with full force, depositing vast quantities of rain and snow on its summits and glaciers. In fact, there are few places on earth where so much precipitation falls in such a short distance and very little moisture reaches the enormous dry plains E of the mountains.

The predictability of TDPNP's weather is further hampered by the existence of numerous micro-climates within the park. The terrain is a complex network of glaciers, rivers, lakes, valleys, mountains and open plains, each of which has an impact on localised weather conditions. Individual mountains, for example, can cause prominent rain shadows, with significant precipitation falling on one side of the mountain and dry, windy weather dominating on the other side. Often weather differs from valley to valley and it is possible therefore to find sunshine on one side of a ridge and cloud/rain over the other side.

This cautionary information is not intended to discourage you but to make you aware of the challenging conditions that you might face and to ensure that you carry clothing and camping gear which can cope with them. The best you can do is to obtain a weather forecast before setting out each day, knowing that there is a good chance that it will not be entirely accurate: as a case in point, apparently forecasts did not predict the blizzard and extreme winds experienced during the 2025 tragedy. Many internet sites and apps provide forecasts, with a varying degree of reliability. The information at **www.mountain-forecast.com** is often well-regarded: it has forecasts for many summits including Cerro Paine Grande and Torre Central. Forecasts are also displayed at refugios/campsites. If you are concerned about a forecast or you are unable to obtain one, then it is sensible to discuss the conditions with staff at the refugios/campsites: their understanding of local weather conditions is often invaluable and you should follow their advice if they tell you it is not safe to hike.

TDPNP entry requirements

All visitors to TDPNP must buy an entrance ticket. You need to purchase it in advance at **www.pasesparques.cl**: we recommend doing this promptly after booking your trip because the website suggests that the park has a maximum capacity. You cannot buy tickets at the park gates. Visitors from overseas pay more than Chilean citizens: currently, a pass for up to 3 days costs US$34; a pass for more than three days costs US$49. You will need to show your ticket when you arrive at the park entrance: you can either provide a printed copy or display it on your mobile device.

Maps

In this book, there are 1:40,000 scale maps for every stage of the treks. Because we were unable to find commercially available maps which fulfilled our requirements, we commissioned our own maps: we believe that these are the finest maps available for TDPNP's treks and they are perfect for navigation on the trail. However, we also recommend obtaining our 1:40,000 scale sheet map for the region, ***Trekking Map: Torres del Paine National Park*** (ISBN 9781912933563): it has the largest scale of any trekking map for TDPNP. Our map makes it easier to plan the trek, identify peaks/features along the trail and navigate in poor conditions. It covers all the treks in TDPNP and can be used seamlessly with this book. It is best to buy this map before leaving home because it is not available in Chile. It is available from **www.knifeedgeoutdoor.com**, online retailers and many shops.

Alternatively, in shops in PN, you will find a confusing array of locally produced maps for TDPNP. Although they come in a variety of different shapes, scales and sizes, the information displayed on each seems to be similar. They are fine for planning but we find that the scale is too small for navigation: accordingly, since most trekkers do most of their planning before arriving in Chile, it is probably better to buy a map before leaving your home country. In any case, the largest scale of the locally available maps is 1:50,000 which is less favourable than the 1:40,000 scale map produced by Knife Edge Outdoor Guidebooks. Perhaps the best of the locally available maps is the 1:50,000 scale map by Cartografía Andesprofundo.

Paths and waymarking

Paths and tracks are generally well-maintained, straightforward to walk upon and simple to follow but occasionally, there are rocky, challenging sections too. The terrain undulates regularly and some sections are steep and/or exposed. Some paths can be muddy and slippery after rain (which is frequent).

Generally, the routes are straightforward to follow in good conditions: there are relatively few trails in TDPNP so you simply stay on the main trail which is usually obvious. Occasionally, there are waymarks (painted on trees/rocks), marker posts and signs to guide the way. From time to time, however, paths are less easy to follow and navigation is more difficult (particularly in bad weather): for example, where the trail crosses rocky zones, it can be faint or disappear completely.

Furthermore, because the paths on the N half of the O are less-trodden than those of the W, often crossing wilder terrain, they can be narrower, rougher and occasionally harder to follow: in particular, the paths of Section 4 (which crosses Paso John Garner) can be tougher than elsewhere and navigation can be challenging in poor weather or low visibility.

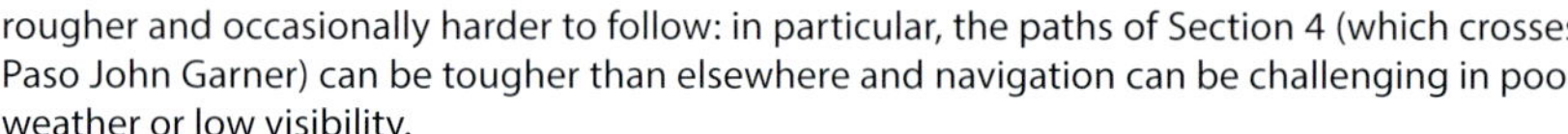

Marker post

In the route descriptions, we do not highlight every junction because the correct route is normally obvious: generally, we only mention junctions if they are particularly significant or if the correct route is not clear. As a rule of thumb, remain on the main path unless instructed otherwise by signs/waymarks on the ground or the maps/route descriptions in this book: however, keep your wits about you because there will, of course, be the occasional exception to this rule! Also, bear in mind that signage and waymarking are at the mercy of the environment: for example, signs and waymarks are sometimes destroyed or concealed by rockfall or snow.

On the high points of TDPNP, snow can remain into early summer, covering paths and making progress/route-finding more difficult: follow waymarks carefully because they can be hard to spot in the snow. Normally, early in the season, the trail will become quickly tracked by others ahead of you but always be wary of following someone else's footprints: although there is a good chance that they are on the correct path, it is obviously possible that they may have strayed from the route. Also, remember that any fresh snow will obscure footprints.

Signpost

Water

Drinking water should be one of your primary considerations each day. Even in the Patagonian mountains, dehydration and sunstroke are possibilities. Tap water at accommodation/campsites is generally drinkable and you should fill up your bottles each morning before you depart: it is good practice to start the day with about 1.5 litres. Along the trail, you can top up water supplies at any huts/campsites you pass or from the many streams/rivers (most of which are shown on our maps): plan carefully so that you know where the next water point is and always check your water levels when you pass a water point.

Remember that the volume of water in streams may vary depending upon the season and the amount of rainfall over previous weeks and months: at the start of the season (November), the rivers are usually in full flow but, by the end of the season (April), some of the smaller ones may be dry. Although some do it, we do not recommend drinking water from a river, stream or lake, without first dealing with possible contaminants including visible particulates, bacteria, viruses, protozoa (for example, giardia) and parasites: although in theory the glacial melt-water should be clean, TDPNP is a busy place with many human visitors whose presence can cause the introduction of contaminants into natural water sources.

It is possible to deal with most contaminants using one or more of the methods described below but you should research thoroughly the specific product you are planning to use to understand its effectiveness and any possible risks:

- **Boiling** is the traditional method. A rolling boil of 1min should kill everything in the water. However, it does not remove visible particulates so the boiled water will remain the same colour as when you found it, which can be off-putting. It also uses up a lot of fuel and takes time so is impractical.
- **Filtering** usually removes visible particulates, working miracles by turning coloured water clear. It also normally removes around 99.9% of bacteria, protozoa and parasites. Filters are often cheap and light. It is the quickest method of treatment so it is useful for long-distance routes. However, most filters cannot remove viruses (although these are unlikely to be an issue in TDPNP): if you are concerned about viruses, then you will need to invest in one of the more expensive (and heavier) filters that remove them or combine filtering with another method (boiling, UV or chemical treatment).
- **Chemical treatment** can remove bacteria, protozoa, viruses and parasites: each product is different so read the labels carefully. However, there are many disadvantages to chemicals: they do not remove visible particulates so the water will remain the same colour as when you found it; water treated with chemicals often has a taste (although you can usually buy additional chemicals to deal with that); the water usually cannot be drunk immediately as chemicals take time to kill pathogens; and from a health perspective, consuming chemicals may not be good for you.
- **UV treatment** kills bacteria, protozoa, viruses and parasites. However, it does not remove visible particulates so the water will remain the same colour as when you found it: coloured water can be off-putting and the UV treatment is less effective if the water is not completely clear. That said, coloured water is not usually a problem on this trek. The most common products are Steripens which are very light.

	Visible Particulates	Bacteria	Virus	Protozoa	Parasites
Boiling	✗	✓	✓	✓	✓
Filter	✓	✓	Only top of the range filters remove viruses	✓	✓
Chemical Treatment	✗	✓	✓	✓	✓
UV Treatment (such as Steripen)	✗	✓	✓	✓	✓

Perhaps the most practical single method for TDPNP is filtering: because virus contamination is unlikely, many hikers drink water which has only been filtered with a standard filter, running a small risk of virus contamination. However, if you prefer to be more cautious, you could buy one of the heavy and expensive filters that deal with viruses. Alternatively, combine filtration with UV treatment (using a Steripen): this should remove or kill practically everything.

The actual effectiveness of individual products varies and is beyond the scope of this book so do your research beforehand. However, it is worth noting that many products claim to be 99.9% effective, indicating that drinking from wild sources cannot be said to be 100% risk free. You will have to weigh the risks and make up your own mind: you drink water at your own risk!

If, like many, you do decide to drink from natural sources then, as well as treating the water, there are a few rules that you should follow to reduce further any risk:

- Avoid water where there is evidence nearby of animals, especially cows or sheep: carcasses (of dead animals) or faeces can cause contamination.
- Do not collect water downstream from buildings or grazing areas.
- Preferably drink from moving water. The faster the better.
- The bigger the river/stream the better.
- Generally the higher the altitude the better.

Storing bags

Some trekkers travel to TDPNP carrying only the gear that they will actually take on the trek. However, most people will have additional baggage which they need to store while trekking. Normally, a hotel that you have stayed at in PN (before the trek) will let you store bags until your return: some may charge extra for this so check when booking. Alternatively, you could use the luggage storage facilities at PN's bus station, Terminal Rodoviario (cash only). Stasher also provides luggage storage facilities in PN (US$4/day; **www.stasher.com**).

Finally, Refugio Grey and Refugio Paine Grande both have luggage rooms where guests can store surplus baggage free of charge. If you were starting and finishing your trek at one of these huts, you could store a bag until your return. However, bear in mind that only one bag (of less than 60 litres) is included in the price of a boat ticket between Pudeto and Paine Grande: an extra bag might therefore incur an additional fee. Central Mountain Hostel also stores bags for US$3/day.

Baggage transfer

Some tour companies can arrange baggage transfer services which deliver your luggage (by car, boat or porter) to the more easily accessible huts/hotels within TDPNP. This spares you from the burden of having to carry a heavy backpack on the trail and enables you to pack more clean clothes and some luxuries. Generally, baggage transfer is only possible for accommodation with vehicle or boat access: Central, PG and Grey. However, some tour companies can also arrange porters that carry bags to Refugio Francés and Refugio Cuernos. There are no baggage transfer services for the more remote huts. At the time of writing, there were no baggage transfer services available for independent trekkers.

Fuel for camping stoves

Airlines will not permit the transport of fuel so campers will need to source it upon arrival in Chile, before setting out on the trek. Generic screw-in gas canisters (which are now pretty much the universal standard) are readily available in shops in PN: outdoor sports stores stock them, as do many other shops. Furthermore, many of the shops at the TDPNP refugios stock screw-in gas canisters (although stocks can run out). If you need petrol/diesel for a multi-fuel stove, there are a number of gas stations in PN. White gas/Coleman fuel is hard to find.

Outdoor shops

There are a number of outdoor shops in PN but stock is often quite limited. Accordingly, it is best to source all your equipment in your home country so that you arrive in Patagonia with all the necessary gear. However, for last-minute gear purchases, you could try the following shops:

- **Volkanica:** this is probably the best outdoor shop in PN, selling gas for stoves, backpacking meals, hiking clothes and camping gear; Hermann Eberhard 532, Puerto Natales; www.volkanica.cl; +56 6 1241 7318.
- **One Aco:** outdoor clothing; Hermann Eberhard 302, Puerto Natales.

Alternatively, in an emergency, you may find some basic clothing and gear in the shop at Central's Welcome Centre.

In PN, you can also rent camping gear at:

- **Rental Natales:** a full camping kit including tent, sleeping bag, sleeping mat, stove, cook-set, trekking poles and backpack costs US$56/day; they also sell freeze-dried backpacking meals; Hermann Eberhard 370, Puerto Natales; www.rentalnatales.com; hola@rentalnatales.com; +56 9 9975 7224.
- **Erratic Rock:** www.erraticrock.com; erraticrock@gmail.com.

Ticks

Ticks are present in Patagonia but they are not generally a serious problem in TDPNP. Even so, check yourself regularly because ticks can carry Lyme disease or tick-borne encephalitis. Remove ticks with a tick removal tool (making sure that you get all of it out) and then disinfect the area.

Drones

The use of drones is not permitted in TDPNP.

Wind safety sign

Equipment

Lago Pehoé

In TDPNP, you will have to carry your own gear unless your tour company can provide a baggage transfer service (see p52). Although you have no influence over challenges like weather and terrain, you do have control over the contents of your pack. Nevertheless, many trekkers set off carrying equipment which is unnecessary or simply too heavy. The more your pack weighs, the harder the trek will be: lugging a pack which is far too heavy can lead to exhaustion, injury and/or abandonment. Accordingly, give equipment choice careful consideration.

Of course, it is easy to understand why a pack should be light, however, it is much more difficult to put this into practice when there are so many things you 'need' in daily life. With experience, it becomes easier to sift between essentials and luxuries but, if you have not been on a multi-day trek before, this can be an unfathomable dilemma. However, if you follow the advice here and limit yourself to the items on our checklist then you should not go far wrong.

A trekker's base weight is the weight of his/her pack, excluding food and water. If you are not carrying camping gear and cooking equipment, it is perfectly possible to get by with a base weight of 5-6kg (13lb) or less. If you intend to carry camping equipment then, by investing in some modern lightweight gear, you could start the trek with a base weight of 8-9kg (17lb) or less. Many people are quick to tell you that the lighter the gear, the greater the price but that is not always the case. While it is true that lightweight gear can be expensive, there are also some excellent lightweight products which are great value. Tents, sleeping bags and backpacks are the three heaviest items that you will carry so they offer the biggest opportunities for weight-saving. But do not ignore the smaller items either as the weight can quickly add up. Accordingly, if your budget permits, it is sensible to invest some money in gear before you leave home. The lighter your gear, the more you will enjoy the trek and the better your chance of success. Be ruthless as every ounce counts.

Recommended basic kit

When undertaking a long-distance route, you should be properly equipped for the worst terrain and the worst weather conditions which you could encounter. In Patagonia, rain is a key consideration (because it is so frequent): you might not get any in practice but you should expect it when planning. Furthermore Patagonia is well-known for its high winds. You should also carry clothing to combat cold: getting cold on a trek is unpleasant and can be dangerous. Furthermore, if you are lucky and the sun does shine, you will want clothing to protect you from it. Also remember that, even in summer, you could experience snow in the mountains.

Layering of clothing is the key to managing body temperature. In cool weather, layers can be added: warm air becomes trapped between the layers, acting as insulation. In warmer weather, you simply remove layers and carry them in your pack. Merino wool or man-made materials are preferable: they are lightweight and warm and they wick moisture away from the skin. Do not wear cotton: it is heavy and it does not dry quickly (making you cold).

Hiking Boots/Shoes	Some use trail-running shoes but others prefer boots with ankle support. They should be good quality, properly fitting and worn in. Robust soles (such as Vibram) are advisable. Shoes/boots with a waterproof membrane (such as Gore-Tex) are a good idea because there is so much rain.	
Socks	Two pairs of good quality, quick-drying walking socks.	
Camp shoes	It is nice to have spare footwear for the evenings. Flip-flops or Crocs are a common choice as they are light. However, if you have comfortable hiking boots/shoes then you might consider not bringing camp shoes to save weight.	
Waterproof jacket and trousers	To provide protection against rain and wind: they should be waterproof and breathable. A mid-weight jacket should be fine: the heaviest material is unnecessary but the lightest fabrics may not provide adequate protection/warmth.	
Base layers	Two T-shirts and underwear: man-made fabrics or merino wool, which wick moisture away from your body.	
Fleece	A warm middle layer. Man-made fabrics are best.	
Trousers/shorts	2 pairs of lightweight walking trousers: convertible trousers are practical as you can remove the legs on warm days. Alternatively, some prefer 1 pair of trousers and 1 pair of shorts.	
Gloves	Lightweight or mid-weight gloves are usually sufficient. However, it is sensible to choose waterproof ones.	
Warm hat & buff	Even in summer, it can be cold in the mountains, particularly on windy days.	
Down jacket	Even in summer, prepare for low temperatures, especially in the evening and early morning.	
Sunglasses, sun hat, sunscreen and lip salve	The sun can be strong: do not set out without these items.	
Head-light with spare batteries	A flashlight is useful (in tents and huts) if you need to go to the bathroom in the night. Furthermore, it is good practice to carry one for emergencies: it can assist if you get caught out late and enables you to signal to rescuers.	

Backpack	Your backpack is one of the heaviest items that you will carry. The difference in the weights of various packs can be surprisingly large. 35-40 litres should be sufficient if you are not carrying camping gear. 50-65 litres should be adequate for campers. If you need a pack bigger than these then you are probably carrying too much. Look for well-padded shoulder straps and waist band. Much of the weight of the pack should sit on your hips rather than your shoulders.
Waterproof pack-liner	Most backpacks are not very waterproof. An internal liner will keep your gear dry if it rains. Many trekkers use external pack covers but we do not find them to be very useful: they flap in the wind and, in heavy rain, water still leaks into the pack around the straps (so you need an internal liner anyway).
Sleeping bag	If you are camping, then you will need your own sleeping bag, unless you have booked a fully-equipped campsite (see p34). If you are staying in dormitories at Vertice's huts, you will need your own sleeping bag (unless you have booked a full bedding kit). At Las Torres huts, full bedding is provided in dormitories so you do not need your own sleeping bag. For further information, on sleeping bags see p57.
Basic first-aid kit	Including plasters (band-aid), a bandage, antiseptic wipes and painkillers. Blister plasters, moleskin padding or tape (such as Leukotape) can be useful to prevent or combat blisters. A tick removal tool/card is also recommended.
Map, compass & GPS device	For maps, see p49. A GPS unit or a smart-phone mapping app is a useful addition but they are no substitute for a map and compass: after all, batteries can run out and electronics can fail.
Walking poles	These transfer weight from your legs onto your arms, keeping you fresher. They also save your knees (particularly on descents) and can reduce the likelihood of falling or twisting an ankle. Poles are invaluable in muddy or snowy conditions.
Phone and charging cable	A smart-phone is a very useful tool on a trek. It can be used for emergencies. Furthermore, apps for weather, mapping and hotel booking are invaluable. It can also serve as your camera, saving weight.
Ziplock plastic bag	A lightweight way of keeping money and passports dry.
Ear plugs	Useful if staying in hut dormitories: you will thank us if someone snores!
Emergency food	Carry some emergency food over and above your planned daily rations. Energy bars, nuts and dried fruit are all good.
Toilet paper and trowel	Bring a lightweight backpacking trowel in case nature calls on the trail: bury toilet waste and carry out used toilet paper.
Whistle	For emergencies. Many rucksacks have one incorporated into the sternum strap.
Knife	A Swiss Army knife for cutting cheese and for emergencies.
Portable battery pack	Although huts/campsites have charging points for electronic devices, they will be in high demand. Accordingly, many people carry portable battery packs. See also p61.

Water bottle	A 1-1.5 litre bottle should suffice because it is not hard to find water along the trail. We like Nalgene wide-mouth bottles because they are light, tough and easy to fill with a filter.
Water filter	We recommend carrying a small water filter to treat stream water sourced along the trail. Katadyn, Sawyer and LifeStraw all make good ones. For more information on water, see p50.
Insect repellent	If the wind dies down, biting bugs can be pesky.
Toiletries	If you wish to take showers at campsites and huts, a small hotel-size bottle of shower gel should be enough to last the trek, saving weight. An almost empty toothpaste tube will also save weight. Leave that make-up behind!
Towel	If you wish to take showers at campsites, you will need to bring a towel: light trekking towels save a lot of weight. If you are staying in a dormitory at Las Torres huts, towels are included in the price, however, there is an additional charge for towels at Vertice huts

Additional backpacking gear

Sleeping bags: to determine whether or not you need to bring your own sleeping bag, see p56. Every sleeping bag has a 'comfort rating': this is the lowest temperature at which the standard woman should enjoy a comfortable night's sleep. There is also a 'lower comfort limit' which is for men. That may sound simple but it is not. Although all reputable sleeping bag manufacturers use the same independent standard, the bags are not tested in the same place so there is a lack of consistency amongst ratings. Also, the ratings are designed with an average man and woman in mind, however, every person is different: some people get colder than others and need a warmer bag. The ratings should therefore be used as a guide only and it is wise to choose a bag with a comfort rating which is at least 5°C lower than the night temperatures that you are likely to encounter.

If you are camping, a bag with a comfort rating between -10°C and 0°C (depending on whether you sleep hot or cold) is normally sufficient to cope with the likely night temperatures for most of the trekking season. However, at the fringes of the season (November/April), it can be prudent to go with something a little warmer in case the weather throws a cold spell at you: perhaps a bag with a comfort rating between -15°C and -5°C. If you plan to use the sleeping bag only in hut dormitories (which are usually slightly warmer than tents), you might choose a bag with a comfort rating which is around 5°C higher than the above suggestions.

It is quite a difficult decision because although you want to be warm at night, you do not want to bring a bag that is much too warm as that would add unnecessary weight to your pack. That said, it is better to be too warm than too cold so err on the side of caution.

Unfortunately, with sleeping bags, price tends to be inversely proportional to weight. This is largely because the lightest bags are filled with goose/duck down which is expensive. Synthetic bags are also available but they are much heavier so down is a better choice for trekking. The disadvantage of down bags is that they can lose their warmth if they get wet but that is less likely if you have a good tent and pack liner. Our advice is first to decide what comfort rating you will require. Then choose the lightest bag (with that rating) which you can afford.

Tent: if you have booked a bare camping pitch (without any rented gear), you will need your own tent. This is one of the heaviest things that you will carry so it provides a big opportunity for weight saving. Some 2-person tents weigh more than 3kg while others weigh less than

0.6kg. The heaviest ones are normally built for extreme winter conditions and are overkill for the normal TDP trekking season. Some of the lightest ones, however, may not be sufficiently robust for TDP where strong winds and heavy rain can batter the tent's outer layer: furthermore, very thin material can be prone to damage on rocky ground.

Although a few premium brands charge a lot for their products and there are some very expensive tents at the lightest end of the scale, these days there are plenty of mid-weight tents available at reasonable prices. Tents weighing 1 to 1.6kg often strike a good balance between price, longevity and weight. Consider money spent here as an investment in your well-being and enjoyment of one of the world's great trails.

Your tent should be waterproof to ensure that you stay dry during rainy nights. A footprint is a good idea to protect its base: 'footprint' is the modern term for what used to be known as a groundsheet. Sometimes you can buy footprints specific to your tent model but we prefer to use a sheet of Tyvek which can be cut to size: Tyvek is extremely tough and is cheaper, and normally lighter, than most branded footprints.

Tent pegs: tent weights provided by manufacturers normally exclude the weight of the pegs. The pegs actually provided with tents can be quite heavy and many trekkers buy replacement ones which are lighter. Six heavy pegs can weigh as much as 240g while 6 light pegs can weigh as little as 6g. There are many different types available these days and it is important to match the peg with the conditions they will be used in. Because it is so windy in TDPNP, pegs need to be strong and thick enough that they do not pull out of the ground easily: titanium ones (which are very light) are a good choice although they can be expensive.

Sleeping mat: if you have booked a bare camping pitch (without any rented gear), you will need your own sleeping mat. A mat makes it comfortable for you to sleep on the hard ground and insulates you from the ground's cold surface. There are three types: air, self-inflating and closed-cell foam. The advantages and disadvantages of each are set out below. All factors considered, we prefer air mats although the very lightest ones may not be sufficiently warm for some trekkers. Thermarest's NeoAir Xlite and NeoAir Xtherm are good choices.

Sleeping mat type	Pros	Cons
Air mats: need to be blown up	Lightest **Very comfortable** Most compact when packed **Thicker: good for side sleepers**	Most expensive **Hard work to inflate** Can be punctured **Less warm than self-inflating**
Self-inflating mats: a combination of air and closed-cell foam. The mat partially inflates itself when the valve is opened	Warmest **Very comfortable** Quite compact **More durable than air mats** Firmness is adjustable by adding air	Heavier **More expensive than closed-cell foam** Can be punctured
Closed-cell foam mats	Light **Least expensive** Most durable **Cannot be punctured**	Not compact: needs to be strapped to the outside of your pack **Least warm** Least comfortable

Pillow: pillows are provided in hut dormitories and fully-equipped camps. However, if you have booked a bare camping pitch or semi-equipped campsite then you will need to bring your own. Some use rolled-up clothing but we prefer inflatable trekking pillows which only weigh around 50g.

Stove: if you plan to cook your own meals, then you will need a backpacking stove. You should choose a stove that uses a type of fuel which is readily available in Patagonia: airlines do not permit you to carry fuel on planes so, if you are flying, you will need to source fuel on arrival (see p53). Because gas is the most widely available fuel, a gas stove is the best choice. Most gas stoves are designed to fit generic screw-on canisters which are readily available in PN and the huts/campsites in TDPNP. Canisters for Campinggaz stoves (which are popular in France) are unlikely to be available. Multi-fuel stoves that burn petrol/diesel are useful but they tend to be heavier, dirtier and more complicated than many gas stoves.

Hundreds of different stoves are available, some more complicated than others. Often the lightest ones are the most simple and often the most simple ones are relatively inexpensive. If, like most campers, you will eat dried food such as pasta and rice then your stove will need to do little more than boil water. A basic stove which mounts on top of a gas canister will therefore be adequate: such a stove should also be cheap and lightweight (less than 100g).

Pots: if, like most campers, you eat dried food such as pasta and rice then you will only need one pot which will do little more than boil water. To save weight, go for the smallest pot that you can get away with. For example, if you are travelling solo and planning to use freeze-dried backpacking meals then you would need nothing bigger than a 500-600ml pot. Titanium pots are usually the lightest but they are slightly more expensive. Get the lightest one that you can afford.

Fork/Spoon: plastic and titanium forks/spoons are usually the lightest: titanium is more expensive but lasts longer. We love Sporks: they have a spoon at one end and a fork at the other. They weigh only 9g and cost very little.

Cuerno Principal

Safety

Cerro Paine Grande

The weather in Patagonia is notoriously unpredictable (see p48). A sudden weather shift or an injury can alter your circumstances dramatically so treat the mountains with respect and be conscious of your experience levels and physical capabilities. The following is a non-exhaustive list of recommendations:

- The fitter you are at the start of your trip, the more you will enjoy the hiking.
- Start hiking early in the day to allow surplus time in case something goes wrong.
- Do not stray from the waymarked paths so as to avoid getting lost and to help prevent erosion of the landscape.
- Before you set out each day, study the route and make plans based upon the abilities of the weakest member of your party.
- Obtain a weather forecast (daily if possible) and reassess your plans in light of it. Avoid exposed routes (especially PJG) if the weather forecast is bad. Also bear in mind that forecasts in Patagonia may not be entirely accurate (see p48.)
- Never be too proud to turn back if you are struggling or if the weather deteriorates.
- Bring a map and compass and know how to use them.
- Carry surplus food and clothing for emergencies.
- Avoid exposed high ground in a thunderstorm. If you get caught out in one then drop your walking poles and stay away from trees, overhanging rocks, metal structures and caves. Generally accepted advice is to squat on your pack and keep as low as possible.
- In snowy conditions, follow markers carefully and do not leave the route. Be wary of following someone else's footprints: there is always a chance that they have strayed from the trail. Always be aware that snow bridges can form over streams and they may not be visible from the surface: if you have any doubts, do not cross.
- Take great care at river/stream crossings: river beds are rocky and uneven and even relatively shallow water can exert a surprisingly strong pull on your legs, knocking you off your feet.
- In the event of an accident, move an injured person into a safe place and administer any necessary first-aid. Keep the victim warm. If possible, use your cell-phone to call for help: the emergency number is 133 (police) or 131 (ambulance service). If you have no signal (which is likely) then send someone to the nearest ranger station/hut/campsite for help.
- When cooking on a camping stove, place the stove on the ground. Avoid using it on a picnic table. We have witnessed a trekker knocking over his stove and spilling boiling water on his legs: this is a sure-fire way to end your trek.

General Information

Language: Spanish is the official language in Chile but the Chilean Spanish actually spoken is a dialect which is very different from the Castilian Spanish used in Spain. Chilean Spanish has a unique speed, rhythm and pronunciation and some of its vocabulary is different. Even some fluent Spanish speakers struggle to understand Chilean Spanish. Fortunately, in most tourist areas, locals will have at least some basic English. And along the trail, it seems that English has largely been adopted as the trekkers' lingua franca.

Charging electronic devices: all accommodation/campsites within TDPNP provide charging facilities. However, in huts/campsites, you sometimes have to queue to use communal power points and therefore many trekkers also bring their own portable battery packs. In Chile, most tourist accommodation provides European two-pin sockets and travellers from outside the EU should get by with a Type-C Europlug adapter. Occasionally, you may encounter Type-L three-pin sockets but they are not very common.

Money: Chile's official currency is the Chilean Peso (CLP). Credit cards are accepted almost everywhere (including all hotels/huts/campsites in TDPNP except for Los Perros). However, there are still a few places where credit cards are not accepted: for example, the Las Torres shuttle bus. Furthermore, it is a good idea to carry some cash in case credit card machines in remote locations are out of order. There are ATMs in PN but none in TDPNP: occasionally, PN's ATMs run out of cash so it is preferable to use the ATMs at Santiago airport before flying to PN.

Visas: citizens of the UK, EU, Australia, New Zealand, Canada or the US do not need a visa for tourist trips to Chile of up to 90 days. On arrival, you are issued with a PDI tourist card which you will need to present upon departure from Chile. If you lose the card, you will have to apply for a duplicate using the PDI platform at **www.serviciomigraciones.cl**.

Cell-phones: there is virtually no cell network in TDPNP. Network is available in most urban areas, including PN. These days, cell networks are usually 4G/5G, enabling access to the internet from smart-phones. However, your cell provider in your home country may charge costly roaming fees if you use the network in Chile: most international trekkers switch off data roaming and use the WiFi at their accommodation instead (see below).

International dialling codes: the country code for Chile is +56.

WiFi: in TDPNP, all hotels, huts and campsites offer WiFi (except for Los Perros and EcoCamp Patagonia). At hotels, it is provided free of charge. However, at huts/campsites, you have to pay to use the WiFi which is expensive, slow and often unreliable: it is managed by external providers and you sign up using one of the on-site machines. Prices start at US$8 for one hour but the hourly rate becomes cheaper if you buy access for a longer period. For example, at Las Torres huts, 3 days' access costs around US$50 and you can use it at any of the Las Torres huts because they are all on the same network. In PN, most accommodation provides free WiFi. WiFi is also provided free of charge on some buses (including many of those operated by Bus-Sur).

Emergencies and rescue: the emergency numbers are 133 (police) and 131 (ambulance service). However, rescue services in Chile are not always free: in particular, helicopter evacuation could cost you a lot of money. Accordingly, it is wise to buy rescue insurance before you leave home. A good option is membership of the British section of the Austrian Alpine Club (which is open to everyone and not just British trekkers): see **www.alpenverein.at/britannia**. Membership costs around £62 and includes worldwide rescue insurance. Note that rescue insurance is different from medical insurance (see below): rescue insurance usually covers only the cost of the rescue itself but not any required medical treatment. Rescue insurance is not usually included with typical travel medical insurance policies: it is normally purchased as an entirely separate policy or as a travel policy add-on.

Medical insurance: medical treatment in Chile is not normally provided free of charge so it is wise to purchase travel medical insurance which covers hiking. Note that medical insurance is different from rescue insurance (see above).

Wildlife

Puma

Within TDPNP's four vegetation zones (see p64), there is an impressive variety of wildlife, although it is often well hidden. There are 25 species of mammals, more than 100 species of birds and a handful of reptiles, amphibians and fish. Generally, early morning is the best time for sightings so get up early if you want to have a chance of ticking off Patagonia's 'big five' (Puma, Guanaco, Huemul, Condor and Rhea).

Mammals

Guanaco: this long-necked camelid is probably the easiest mammal to spot. They are native to South America and look much like a llama (a close relation). They graze in herds on TDPNP's wide grassy plains. The Q Extension is good for guanaco sightings (see p120).

Guanaco

Puma: see image above. This is the park's apex predator. Everyone wants to spot one but few ever do. They can live almost everywhere (even in the forests) and usually prey on the park's guanacos: however, they will also eat livestock given half the chance. Although TDPNP is thought to be the best place in Patagonia to spot them, your chances of seeing one are small. But just because you cannot see them, does not mean that they are not watching you!

Huemul

Huemul (South Andean deer): although this endangered deer is pictured on Chile's national coat of arms, it is even harder to spot in the wild than the puma. It has a brown coat and lives in TDPNP's thick forests. Although it was once found across much of Chilean Patagonia, it was hunted almost to extinction and it is estimated that there are only 1500-2000 huemuls remaining in the wild.

Geoffroy's cat

Geoffroy's cat: a spotted nocturnal cat which is the size of a house cat and has a coat much like a leopard's. It feeds on rodents and small birds and is extremely hard to spot.

Dwarf (Pichi) armadillo: they inhabit TDPNP's grasslands, eating ants, scorpions and beetles.

Fox: TDPNP has two types of fox. The cupleo fox (which is red in colour) inhabits forests, deserts and high plateaus. The southern grey fox (which is obviously grey) is often seen on TDPNP's plains.

Hog-nosed skunk: they inhabit TDPNP's grasslands, eating insects and rodents. They are easiest to spot at dawn and dusk (when they are most active).

Birds

Caracara

Andean condor: this black and white vulture is generally considered to be the world's largest bird of prey. It has a wingspan of up to 3.3m and can weigh up to 15kg. It is a scavenger which feeds on carrion. Along with the huemul, it is pictured on Chile's coat of arms. TDPNP has plenty of condors so you have a very good chance of spotting one, soaring in the thermals near cliffs and crags. However, if you want to see them close up, Mirador Condor is hard to beat (see p128).

Rhea

Southern crested caracara: this bird of prey is the world's second largest falcon. It can tolerate a range of different environments and there are plenty in TDPNP. It feeds mainly on carcasses of dead animals but will also seize small live prey.

Darwin's rhea (ñandu): this flightless bird is similar in size and appearance to the ostrich. It lives on Patagonia's grasslands, feeding on both plants and insects.

Magellanic woodpecker

Chilean flamingo: this gorgeous pink bird inhabits Patagonia's salt lakes, lagoons and fjords. You can often spot them in Laguna Amarga.

Magellanic woodpecker: you are likely to hear this beautiful bird before you see it because, like all woodpeckers, it hammers its beak against the trunks of trees. They all have jet black bodies but the males possess a spectacular crimson head whereas the females' heads are predominantly black. You can spot them in TDPNP's beech forests.

Austral pygmy owl

Austral parakeet: the world's southernmost parrot has predominantly green plumage with dull reddish patches on its belly and tail. They live in TDPNP's beech forests.

Austral pygmy owl: this small owl lives in and around TDPNP's forests. It feeds on mice, insects and other birds. Unlike many owls, it can be spotted during the day. Look out for them on Sections 2 and 3.

Condor

Plants & Flowers

TDPNP has four main vegetation zones:

Pre-Andean shrubland: occupying most of TDPNP, this zone of hardy evergreen shrubs is found on plains and plateaus (frequently near lakes and rivers). The plants can store a lot of water and are able to survive challenging weather. Common plants include:

- **Chilean firebush (notro):** see image above. Every trekker wants to see this evergreen tree in bloom. It produces clusters of vibrant red flowers which cover many slopes in spring and early summer. You will find it on sections 6, 7 and 8 (between PG and Central).

Calafate

- **Box-leaved barberry (calafate):** this evergreen shrub is a berberis native to Chile/Argentina. It has small blue-black berries which are edible. Legend has it that anyone who eats a calafate berry will once again return to Patagonia.

Magellanic deciduous forest: dense, ancient forest of **Lenga** (nothofagus pumilio; see p82), **Ñirre** (nothofagus antarctica) and **Coihue** (nothofagus dombeyi), which are all types of beech trees. The Andes trap moisture from the prevailing Pacific winds, creating a humid environment in which beech trees thrive. Lenga and Ñirre are deciduous trees which are found at higher altitudes whereas Coihue is an evergreen beech found at lower elevations. Amongst the trees, look for the following:

Misodendrum

- **Misodendrum:** pale green parasitic plants grow on the beech trees as mistletoes. They are hemi-parasites native only to South America.
- **Darwin's fungus (Indian bread):** bright orange balls of fungus which grow on the trees' branches.
- **Old man's beard:** a stringy lichen which hangs from the trees' branches.
- **Fuchsia:** a tall shrub producing striking red flowers which dangle downwards from the branches. Cultivated fuchsia is also found in domestic gardens around the world.

Darwin's fungus

Patagonian steppe: vast, open, semi-arid plains of tuft grasses and low shrubs with low-rise mountains, river valleys and canyons. The vegetation is battered by the fierce Patagonian winds so there are few trees. The sandy/stony soil is of poor organic quality. Common plants include:

- **Black shrub (mata negra):** a small evergreen shrub with narrow grey-green leaves and white flowers. It was first documented during Captain Cook's second voyage in 1774.
- **Guanaco bush (neneo macho):** a low 'cushion' shrub with silvery-green leaves. Fiery red-orange flowers cover the plant in spring.

Andean desert: high altitude areas of sparse vegetation which have no tall trees. The hardy plants (like dwarf shrubs and succulents) are perfectly adapted to cold and heavy rain. Look out for **devil's strawberry**, a low growing herb with shiny kidney-shaped leaves and red berries (which are edible but not pleasant).

Lago Grey

Route Descriptions

The view from Mirador Condor

1 Central to Serón (O/Q)

Starting from Central, the first stage of the O seems perfectly pitched: difficult enough to test your legs before the tougher challenges later in the trek but not so hard that you will finish the day overly exhausted. And the scenery is spectacular enough to thrill without revealing all of TDP's treasures too soon, leaving plenty of delights and surprises for subsequent days. Those starting the O at PG should, by now, be 'trail-hardened' and Section 1 should seem easier then the previous few days (which have more climbing/descent).

The route climbs NE from Central around the slopes of Cerro Paine (not to be confused with Cerro Paine Grande, TDPNP's highest peak) until you are high above Río Paine which loops gracefully back and forth along the floor of the valley below. This section of the route offers good views of the Towers (to the W). To the SW, you will spot the huge Lago Nordenskjöld: both the O and the W follow the entire N side of the lake on Section 7. From the NE side of Cerro Paine, the route descends N to the valley floor and follows Río Paine all the way to the magnificent plateau that is home to the remote Serón campsite.

	Start	Finish	Time	Distance	Ascent (ACW)	Descent (ACW)	Max Alt
1	Central	Serón	4:30	14.1km 8.8miles	334m 1096ft	304m 997ft	390m 1280ft

Serón campsite

Central is a fragmented and confusing place. The shuttle bus from LA drops off at the car park beside the Welcome Centre: from there, a path leads W to Central Mountain Hostel (2-3min). Another path leads W from the hostel to Central Campsite (5min; for directions, see p71). Hotel Las Torres is 10min SW of the campsite (for directions, see p115).

Terrain	Good paths/tracks which are straightforward to follow.
Route-finding	Straightforward: always remain on the main path, ignoring offshoots.
Accommodation/ Camping	**Serón** (operated by Las Torres): camping only (bare tent pitches; semi-equipped/equipped fixed tents).
Meals/Drinks	**Serón:** breakfast, dinner & drinks. Boxed lunches to go also available.
Supplies	**Serón:** small shop selling only basic snacks/drinks (see image on p41)
Trail notes	At Serón, there is a well-preserved old cart which provides evidence of the region's rural history (see image above).
Points of Interest	Views of the E side of the Towers Río Paine Lago Nordenskjöld
Transport	**Central:** shuttle bus to/from LA. Central's bus stop is at the car park beside the Welcome Centre.

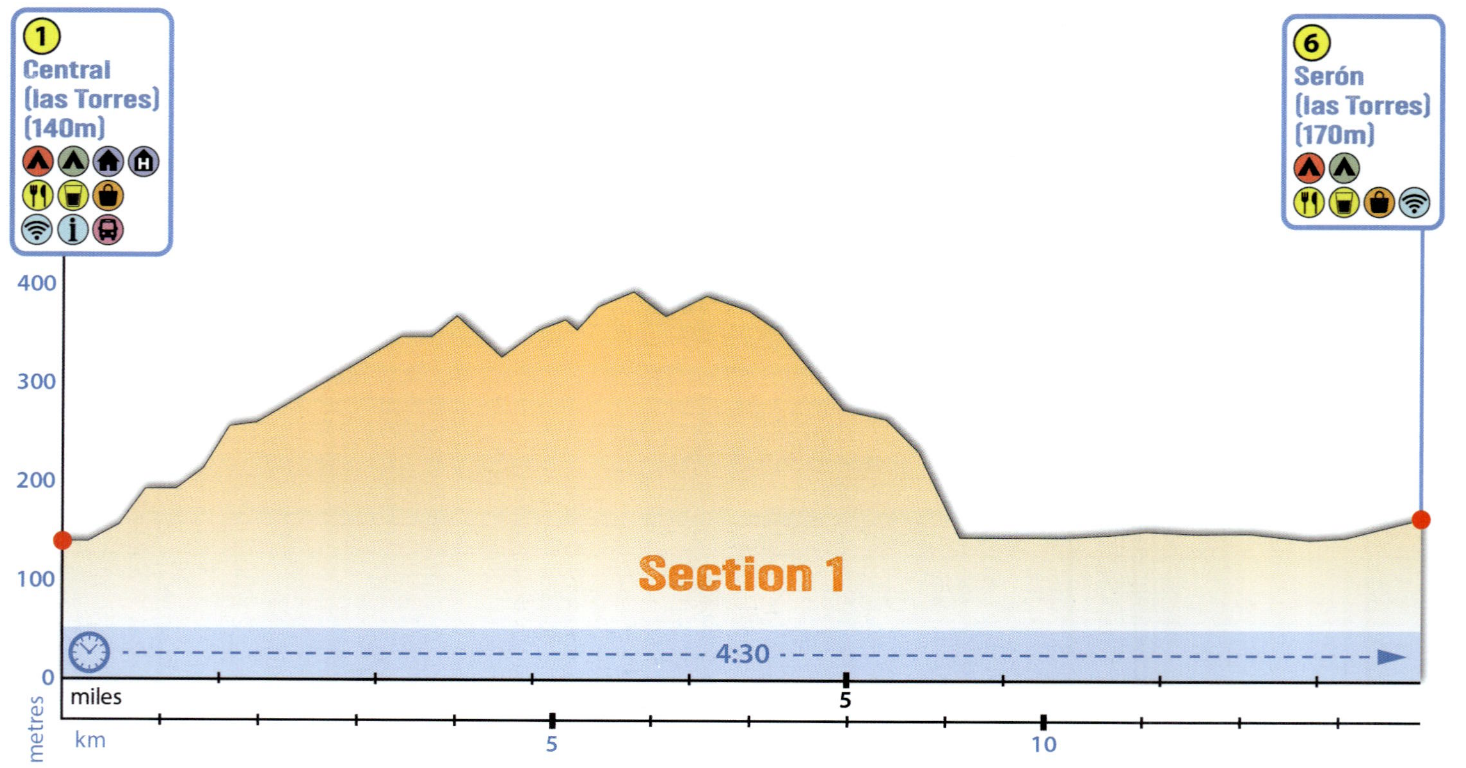
1
Central
(las Torres)
(140m)
6
Serón
(las Torres)
(170m)
400
300
200
100
0
metres
Section 1
4:30
miles
5
km
5
10

Stage 1: Central to Serón

1 See map on p72. From the **Welcome Centre**, follow a path W, parallel to the vehicle track. A few minutes later, keep SH at a junction: alternatively, TR for **Central Mountain Hostel**. Shortly afterwards, the path bends right to head N ('Serón'): the track heading W goes to **Central Campsite**. Shortly afterwards, TR onto a track: alternatively, head W on a path for **Central Campsite**. Shortly after that, at another junction, keep SH on a broad track ('Serón'). Soon, TR at a junction of tracks.

2 0:20: At a junction, keep SH across a cattle grid: alternatively, TR for **EcoCamp Patagonia**. Just afterwards, TL onto a grassy path: ignore any offshoots, staying on the main path. Soon climb steeply. Keep SH across a beautiful viewpoint: afterwards, the path heads through an enclosed gully.

3 0:40: From a junction, keep SH for the main path; alternatively, TR onto a narrow path to visit an excellent viewpoint; if you continue N from that viewpoint, you will soon rejoin the main path. Soon head through a section of woodland.

4 2:40: Cross a stream. As you descend into the valley, there are spectacular views of Río Paine's loops.

5 3:15: See map on p75. Near the base of the valley, TR and cross a stile. A few minutes later, cross a bridge. 10min later, cross another bridge. 15min later, cross a stream. Soon afterwards, the path finally meets the river and follows it N. When the river bends E, follow the path N (away from it).

6 4:30: Arrive at **Serón Campsite (170m)**.

Río Paine

Cerro Paine
1467
uardería Torres
Chileno
(las Torres)
(410m)
Stage 8a
Río Ascencio
Windy Pass
471
Central
Campsite
Hotel
Las Torres
Stage 8b
Stage 7b
Central
Mountain
Hostel
Cuernos-Central
Direct Route

Río Paine
Cascada del Paine
tage 1
coCamp Patagonia
Stage 0
1
Central
(las Torres)
(140m)
elcome
entre
Laguna Amarga

Lago
8
Coirón Ranger Station
Stage 2
1662
Paine Lookout
Oggioni

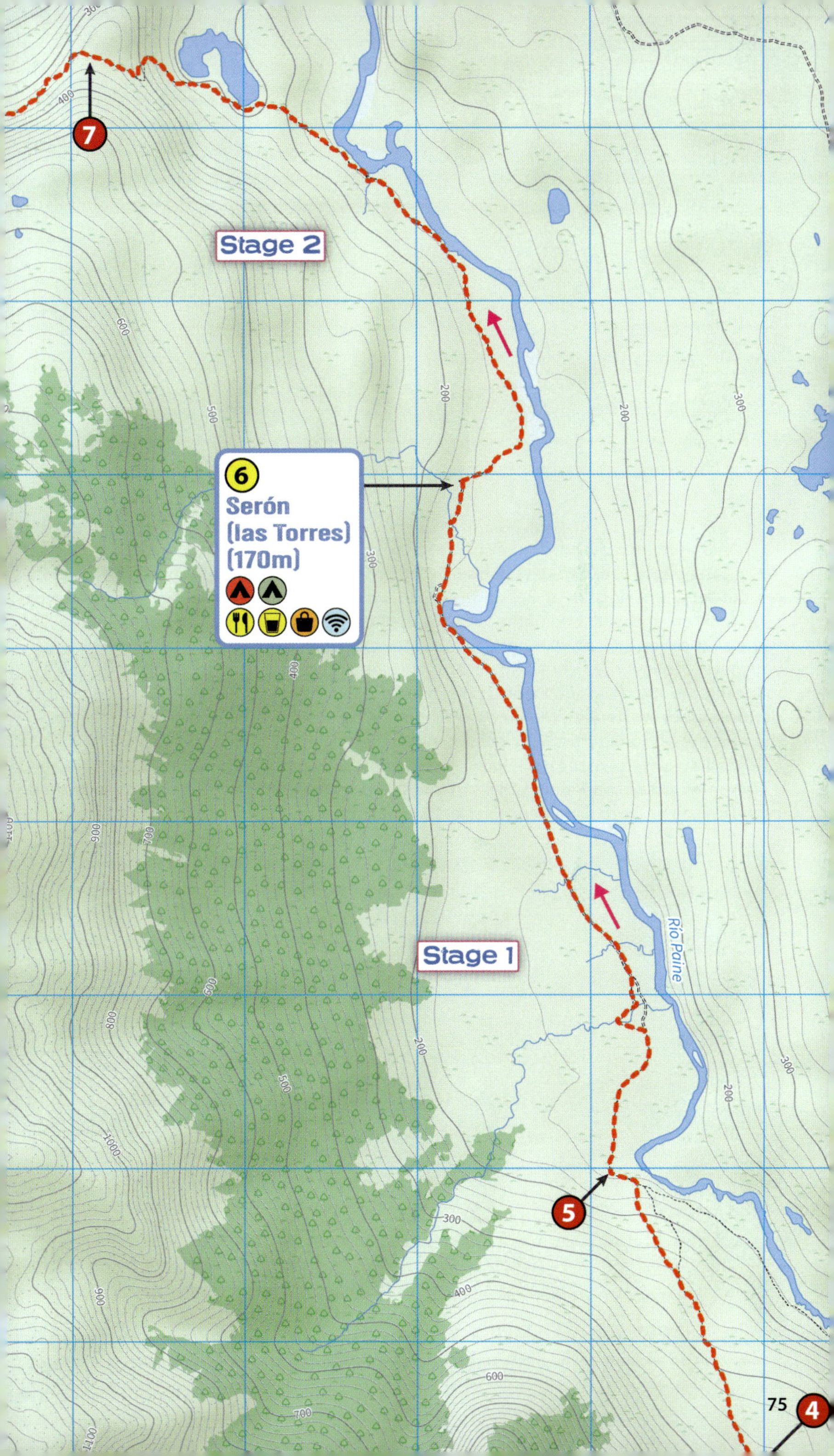

Stage 2
6
Serón
(las Torres)
(170m)
Stage 1
Río Paine
7
5
4

2 Serón to Dickson (O/Q)

Lago Dickson

This long section of the O cannot be shortened in any way: only Section 6 is longer and it can be split over two days. It is an exceptionally beautiful hike through TDPNP's most remote terrain. It finishes at Refugio Dickson which is set spectacularly on the shores of Lago Dickson: at the far end of the lake, lies the huge Glacier Dickson. The route follows Río Paine all the way, except where the river is interrupted by Lago Paine. After leaving Serón, you initially follow the river N: however, after climbing over a spur, the path undulates W, following the shore of Lago Paine; you pick up the river again at the lake's W side. For most of this journey westwards, the views are stunning, with snowy peaks and glaciers drawing the eye: the outlook to the W is consistently excellent but, for long periods, you will also enjoy fabulous views of the main Paine Massif to the S. Eventually, the route deposits you on a viewpoint just above Refugio Dickson and this is the highlight of the day: you look N up Lago Dickson to Cerro Ohnet and Glaciers Dickson and Cubo.

Terrain	In good conditions, the clear paths are usually straightforward to negotiate, however, they can be muddy and slippery after rain. Occasionally, the route is quite steep. The distance to cover is long (18.3km) so this is a tiring section.
Route-finding	Straightforward: always remain on the main path, ignoring offshoots.
Accommodation/ Camping	**Dickson** (operated by Vertice): mixed dormitories; camping (bare tent pitches; tents, sleeping bags and mattresses for rent).
Meals/Drinks	**Dickson:** breakfast, lunch, dinner & drinks. Boxed lunches available.
Supplies	**Dickson:** a well-stocked shop sells basic food/snacks/drinks.
Points of Interest	Río Paine, Lago Paine, Lago Dickson and Glacier Dickson. Views of the N side of the main Paine Massif.
Transport	None.

	Start	Finish	Time	Distance	Ascent (ACW)	Descent (ACW)	Max Alt
2	Serón	Dickson	5:50	18.3km 11.4miles	455m 1493ft	415m 1362ft	361m 1184ft

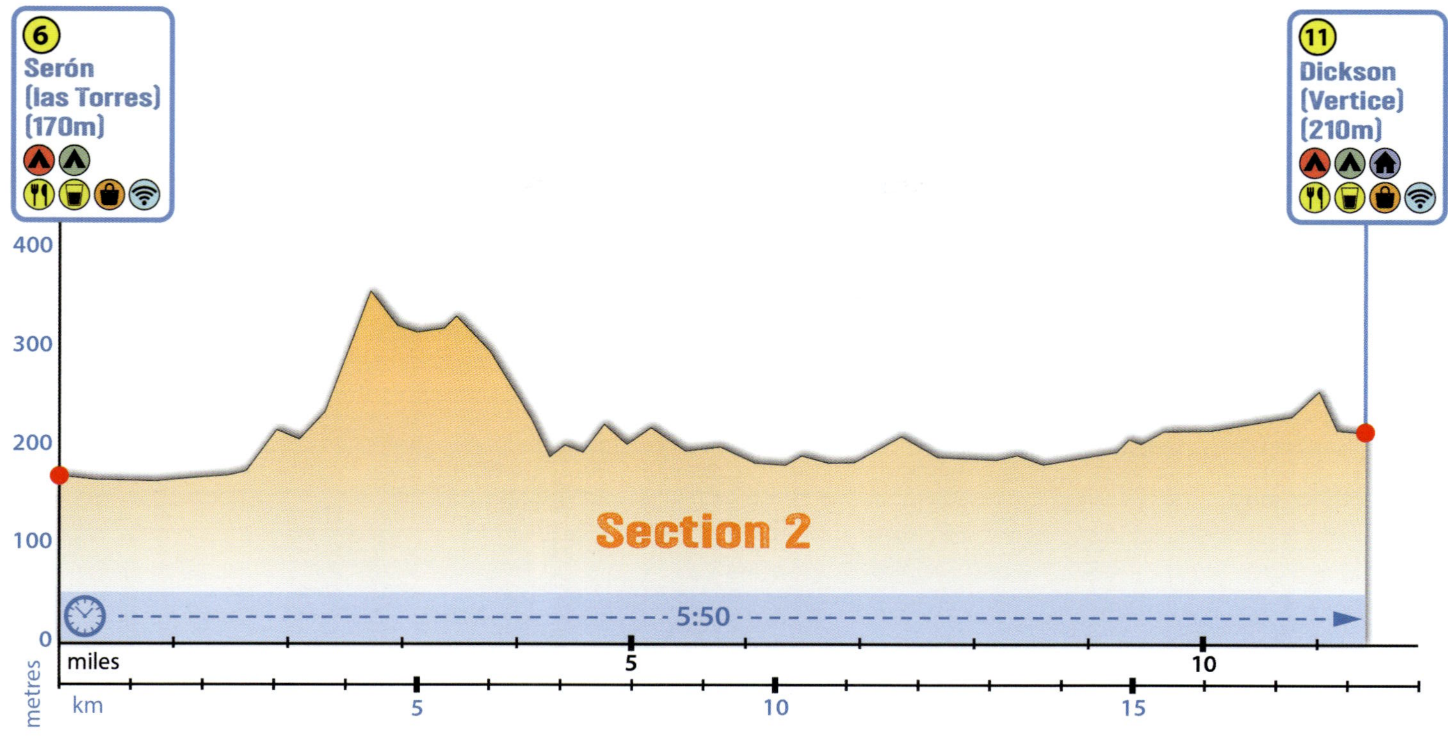
6
Serón
(las Torres)
(170m)
11
Dickson
(Vertice)
(210m)
400
300
200
100
0
metres
Section 2
5:50
miles
5
10
km
5
10
15

11
Dickson (Vertice) (210m)
Stage 3
10
Río de los Peros
Mirador del Valle d
Stage 3
13
14
15
condido
1457

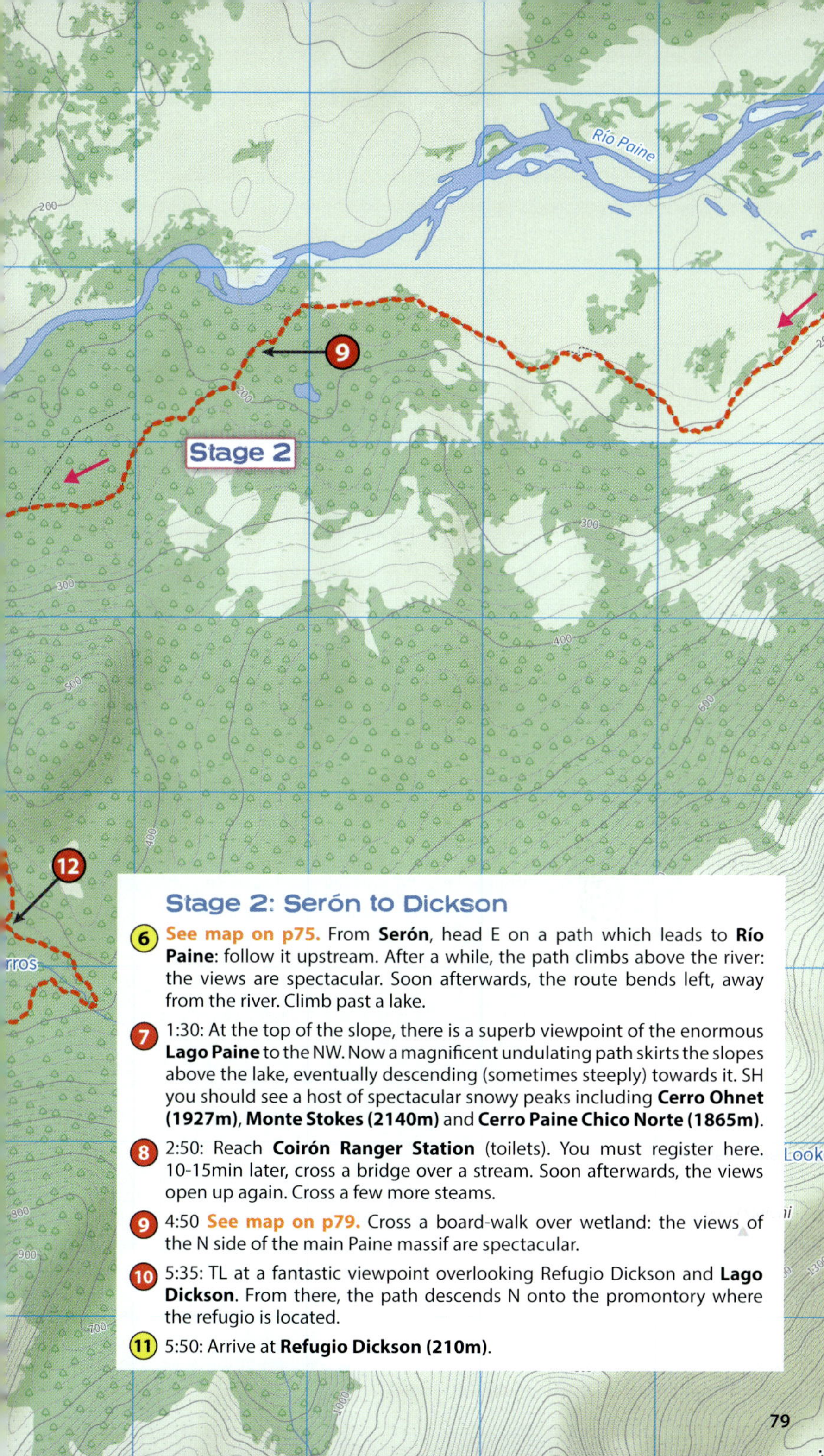

Stage 2: Serón to Dickson

6 **See map on p75.** From **Serón**, head E on a path which leads to **Río Paine**: follow it upstream. After a while, the path climbs above the river: the views are spectacular. Soon afterwards, the route bends left, away from the river. Climb past a lake.

7 1:30: At the top of the slope, there is a superb viewpoint of the enormous **Lago Paine** to the NW. Now a magnificent undulating path skirts the slopes above the lake, eventually descending (sometimes steeply) towards it. SH you should see a host of spectacular snowy peaks including **Cerro Ohnet (1927m)**, **Monte Stokes (2140m)** and **Cerro Paine Chico Norte (1865m)**.

8 2:50: Reach **Coirón Ranger Station** (toilets). You must register here. 10-15min later, cross a bridge over a stream. Soon afterwards, the views open up again. Cross a few more steams.

9 4:50 **See map on p79.** Cross a board-walk over wetland: the views of the N side of the main Paine massif are spectacular.

10 5:35: TL at a fantastic viewpoint overlooking Refugio Dickson and **Lago Dickson**. From there, the path descends N onto the promontory where the refugio is located.

11 5:50: Arrive at **Refugio Dickson (210m)**.

3 Dickson to Los Perros (O/Q)

Lenga beech forest

A world class trek requires variety of terrain and Section 3 delivers this by exploring one of the most forested places in TDPNP. In other parts of the park, wild-fires have ravaged the vegetation but here the native Lenga beech forest is pristine (see p82). It is an atmospheric wonderland of moss-covered tree trunks, thick green vegetation and fast-flowing torrents, where Magellanic woodpeckers and Austral parakeets thrive: on our most recent visit, we even spotted an Austral pygmy owl in broad daylight.

Of course, forest exploration requires that you spend time below the tree-line, forgoing far-reaching views for a while. However, Section 3 does not keep you hidden away throughout because, 1hr from Rifugio Dickson, you pop out above the trees at Mirador del Valle de Los Perros: this is a fabulous viewpoint (beside Cerro Paine Chico Norte) which looks N onto Lago and Glacier Dickson and W along the Los Perros valley. Furthermore, about 1.5km before Camping Los Perros, the trail leaves the trees again and delivers spectacular views of Glacier Los Perros and the surrounding peaks.

Camping Los Perros is located at the edge of the forest, under cover of trees. Its remote location means that facilities are limited: showers are cold and there is no restaurant. Because Section 3 is short, many trekkers find that they reach Los Perros quite early in the day. If weather permits, a visit to the beautiful Mirador Glaciar Los Perros (on the N side of Laguna Los Perros) is a lovely way to pass the time. However, in bad weather, Los Perros is a dank place to spend the afternoon.

Itinerary options: because Section 3 is short, fit trekkers may wish to combine it with Section 4 (which heads over PJG): bear in mind though that Section 4 is the toughest, and most exposed, part of the O so do not plan to double up the Sections unless you are sure that it is within your capabilities. Alternatively, you could combine Sections 2 and 3 although this also makes for a very long day. In either case, because you are required to book a night at both Dickson and Los Perros, you would have to pay for a night that you do not ultimately use: fortunately, Vertice's campsites are inexpensive. **Note that after the 2025 tragedy (p2), a new rule was introduced, limiting the number of people crossing PJG each day to 100: at the date of press, it was not yet clear what impact (if any) this limit would have on the ability to double-up stages.**

	Start	Finish	Time	Distance	Ascent (ACW)	Descent (ACW)	Max Alt
3	Dickson	Los Perros	3:50	11.9km 7.4miles	473m 1552ft	118m 387ft	580m 1903ft

Terrain	Much of Section 3 lies below the tree-line. Paths are rougher than on Sections 1 and 2: plenty of rocks and roots; muddy and slippery after rain. Some sections are quite steep.
Route-finding	Between 13 and Los Perros 16, the path can be tricky to follow over rocks/roots. Otherwise, navigation is straightforward: always remain on the main path, ignoring offshoots.
Accommodation/ Camping	**Los Perros** (operated by Vertice): camping only (bare tent pitches; tents, sleeping bags and mattresses for rent); cold showers only.
Meals/Drinks	No meals available.
Supplies	**Los Perros:** the small shop sells candy bars/drinks. Often no other food is available so bring your own.
Trail notes	No WiFi or cell reception at Los Perros.
Points of Interest	Mirador del Valle de Los Perros: views of Lago Dickson, Glacier Dickson and the Los Perros valley. Glacier Los Perros. Views of Paso John Garner.
Transport	None.

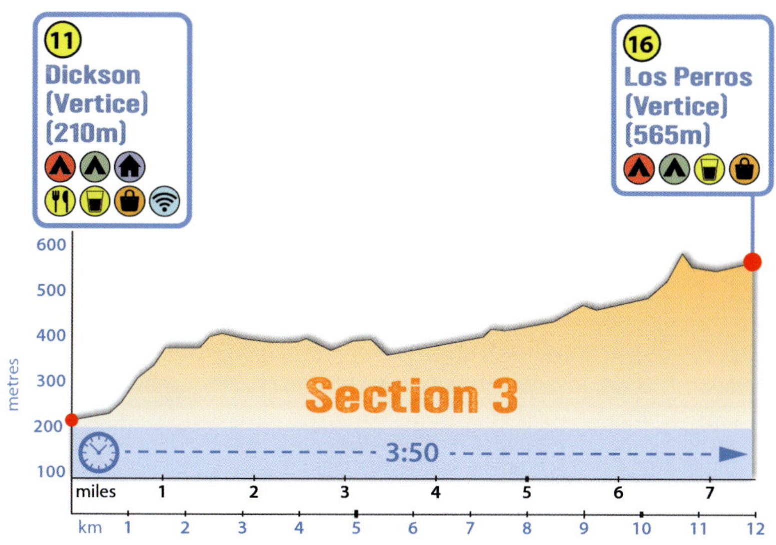

Lenga Beech Woodland

The Lenga beech (nothofagus pumilio) is a deciduous tree/shrub native to the southern Andes. It can grow up to 30m high with a maximum trunk diameter of 1.5m. The green, elliptical, toothed leaves are 2-4cm long and they turn to yellow/red in autumn. The fruit of the tree is a small nut. It prefers cold climates with plenty of snow and can normally regenerate quickly after fires.

Stage 3: Dickson to Los Perros

11 See map on p78. From **Refugio Dickson**, follow a path SW into forest ('Los Perros'). Soon the route bends left and climbs steeply S. After an initial steep ramp, the path undulates relentlessly through the forest.

12 1:20: Reach **Mirador del Valle de Los Perros**. 15 min later, cross a bridge over a fast river. 45min later, cross another bridge over a stream.

13 2:55: Cross a bridge over a raging torrent. There are superb views of **Glacier Los Perros** (on the left). Afterwards, the path can be hard to follow over rocks/roots. 15-20min later, cross another bridge: after it, the path is slightly unclear. When the path emerges from the trees, follow orange posts across rocks: watch your step.

14 See map on p83. The path climbs to a spectacular viewpoint overlooking **Glacier Los Perros** and **Laguna Los Perros**. From there, descend W.

15 3:35: TR at a junction: alternatively, TL for a viewpoint of the glacier. Afterwards, you can spot **PJG** (to the W) which you will cross on Section 4.

16 3:50: Pass **Los Perros ranger station** (where you must register). Shortly afterwards, reach **Camping Los Perros (565m)**.

23 Puente John Gardner

4 Los Perros to Grey (O/Q)

On a fine day, this is one of the most spectacular parts of the O. However, it is also one of the trek's most challenging sections because you start the day with its longest and most difficult climb: immediately after departure from Los Perros, the trail starts upwards and does not relent until you reach Paso John Garner (the O's highest point). As soon as you rise above the tree-line, the views are fantastic but the panorama from PJG is nothing short of staggering: you find yourself a mere stone's throw from the gargantuan Glacier Grey and the snowy peaks behind it. It is the largest glacier in TDPNP and its scale is mind-blowing: 28km long, 6km wide and 30m high (on average). You cannot actually see it until you approach the top of the pass, where it is suddenly revealed with breath-taking effect.

The glacier views continue as you descend W off PJG and, even after you dip below the tree-line again, there are numerous viewpoints that will make your jaw drop. The path continues S all the way to Refugio Grey, flanking the glacier until its snout meets the icy waters of Lago Grey and then running alongside the lake: on the way, you cross three exhilarating suspension bridges across steep-sided gorges.

At the end of Section 4, there is dormitory accommodation and camping at Refugio Grey: it is a modern structure, built in 2012, with a good restaurant/bar (serving pizzas/burgers throughout the afternoon). Because Refugio Grey is where the O meets the W, it is a busy place: this can be a shock to the system for OTs who have been used to quieter trails over the previous days. Mid-section, you pass Guarderia Paso which used to have a campsite: this provided a useful way of breaking up Section 4 but unfortunately, it closed a few years ago. We recently spoke to the rangers there who told us that camping may again be possible in the future.

	Start	Finish	Time	Distance	Ascent (ACW)	Descent (ACW)	Max Alt
4a	Los Perros	Paso	4:00	8.5km 5.3miles	682m 2238ft	780m 2559ft	1180m 3872ft
4b	Paso	Grey	2:15	7.0km 4.4miles	183m 600ft	580m 1903ft	481m 1578ft

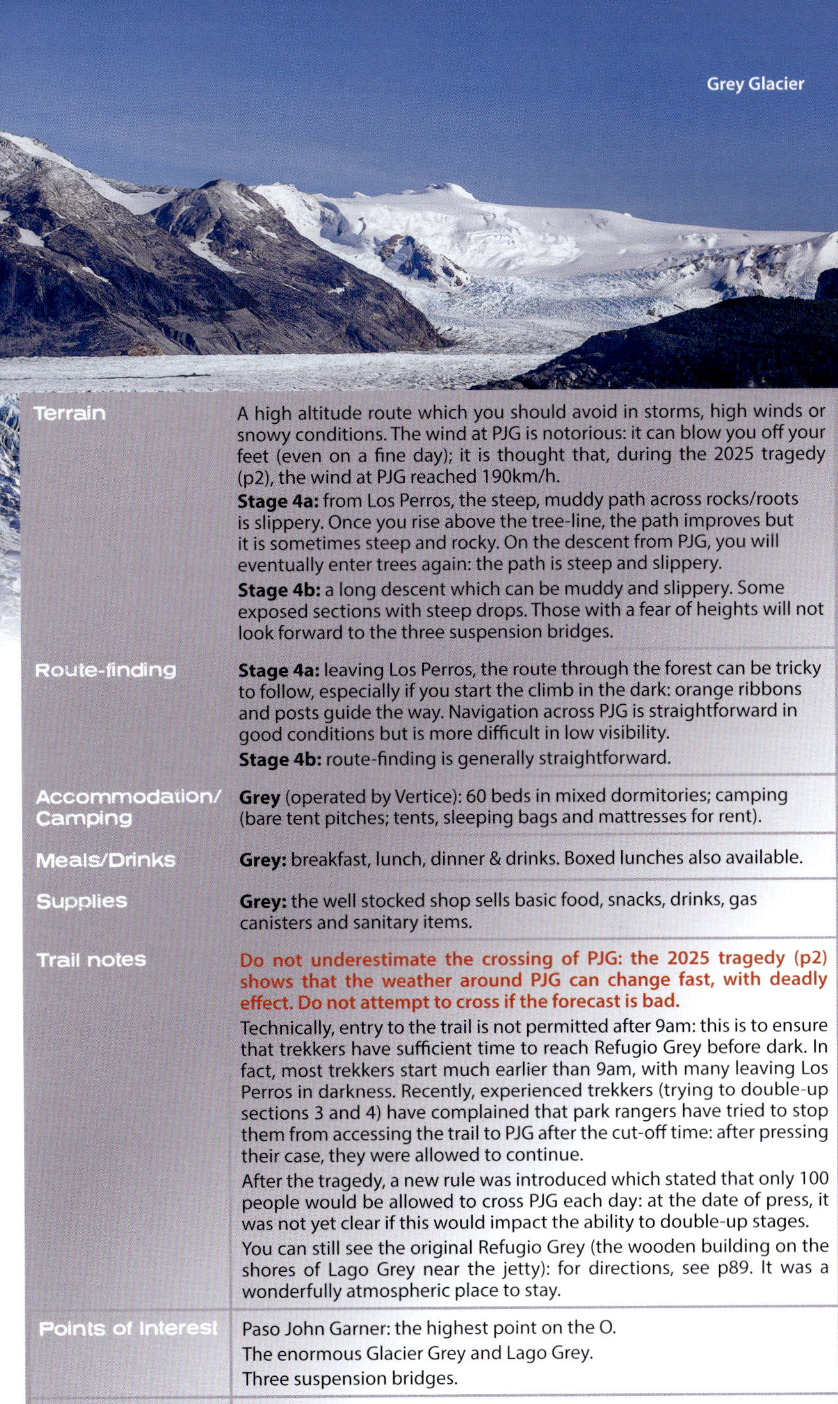

Grey Glacier

Terrain	A high altitude route which you should avoid in storms, high winds or snowy conditions. The wind at PJG is notorious: it can blow you off your feet (even on a fine day); it is thought that, during the 2025 tragedy (p2), the wind at PJG reached 190km/h. **Stage 4a:** from Los Perros, the steep, muddy path across rocks/roots is slippery. Once you rise above the tree-line, the path improves but it is sometimes steep and rocky. On the descent from PJG, you will eventually enter trees again: the path is steep and slippery. **Stage 4b:** a long descent which can be muddy and slippery. Some exposed sections with steep drops. Those with a fear of heights will not look forward to the three suspension bridges.
Route-finding	**Stage 4a:** leaving Los Perros, the route through the forest can be tricky to follow, especially if you start the climb in the dark: orange ribbons and posts guide the way. Navigation across PJG is straightforward in good conditions but is more difficult in low visibility. **Stage 4b:** route-finding is generally straightforward.
Accommodation/ Camping	**Grey** (operated by Vertice): 60 beds in mixed dormitories; camping (bare tent pitches; tents, sleeping bags and mattresses for rent).
Meals/Drinks	**Grey:** breakfast, lunch, dinner & drinks. Boxed lunches also available.
Supplies	**Grey:** the well stocked shop sells basic food, snacks, drinks, gas canisters and sanitary items.
Trail notes	**Do not underestimate the crossing of PJG: the 2025 tragedy (p2) shows that the weather around PJG can change fast, with deadly effect. Do not attempt to cross if the forecast is bad.** Technically, entry to the trail is not permitted after 9am: this is to ensure that trekkers have sufficient time to reach Refugio Grey before dark. In fact, most trekkers start much earlier than 9am, with many leaving Los Perros in darkness. Recently, experienced trekkers (trying to double-up sections 3 and 4) have complained that park rangers have tried to stop them from accessing the trail to PJG after the cut-off time: after pressing their case, they were allowed to continue. After the tragedy, a new rule was introduced which stated that only 100 people would be allowed to cross PJG each day: at the date of press, it was not yet clear if this would impact the ability to double-up stages. You can still see the original Refugio Grey (the wooden building on the shores of Lago Grey near the jetty): for directions, see p89. It was a wonderfully atmospheric place to stay.
Points of Interest	Paso John Garner: the highest point on the O. The enormous Glacier Grey and Lago Grey. Three suspension bridges.
Transport	Boats between Refugio Grey and HLG (see p45). The jetty at Refugio Grey is 0.6km on foot from reception (for directions, see p89).

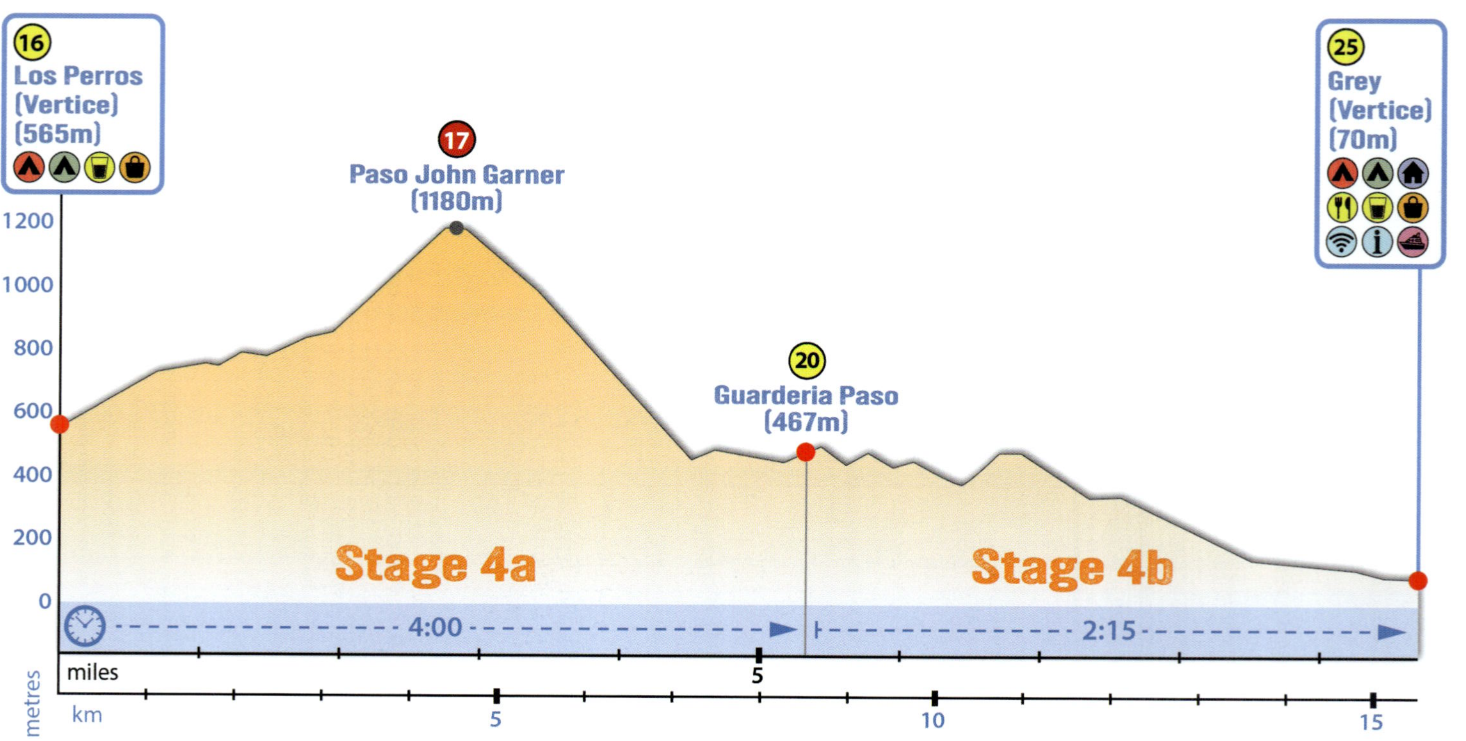
16
Los Perros
(Vertice)
(565m)
17
Paso John Garner
(1180m)
20
Guarderia Paso
(467m)
25
Grey
(Vertice)
(70m)
1200
1000
800
600
400
200
0
metres
Stage 4a
Stage 4b
4:00
2:15
miles
5
km
5
10
15

Stage 4a: Los Perros to Paso

16 **See map on p83.** From **Camping Los Perros**, climb on a challenging trail through the forest. After 1.5km, reach a spectacular viewpoint: you can now clearly see PJG. Afterwards, descend briefly into trees again. Then follow a rocky path which contours around the slopes. Soon leave the trees behind and climb WSW across the barren rocky slopes: the higher you climb, the closer you get to the spectacular glacier beneath **Cerro Amistad** and **Cerro Cóndor**.

17 2:45: Cross **Paso John Garner (1180m)**. Over the other side, the views of **Glacier Grey** will blow you away (and there is a risk that the wind could do so too!). Keep SH and descend W towards the glacier.

18 3:15: At about 950m, the path enters forest and the trees provide shelter from the wind. Take care descending steep, muddy steps. After a long knee-jarring descent, the path undulates relentlessly S, still within the trees.

19 3:55: Cross a bridge over a torrent.

20 4:00: Arrive at **Guarderia/Campamento Paso**. You need to register here.

Stage 4b: Paso to Grey

20 **See map on p82.** From **Guarderia/Campamento Paso**, continue S through the forest. 5min later, reach a fabulous viewpoint overlooking **Glacier Grey**.

21 0:30: Cross an amazing suspension bridge. Afterwards, descend steeply: the trail undulates alongside the glacier.

22 1:00 TL at a junction. Shortly afterwards, cross another suspension bridge.

23 1:30: Cross a third suspension bridge: take care descending the ladder at the far side of it. **See map on p89.** 5-10min later, reach another fabulous viewpoint.

24 2:10: Keep SH at a junction: the path to the right leads to **Mirador Grey** (p88) and the boat jetty (p89).

25 2:15: Shortly afterwards, pass the campsite to reach the reception area at **Refugio/Camping Grey (70m)**.

View of Cerro Amistad on the approach to PJG

Mirador Grey

25min; 1.5km (return trip from Refugio Grey)

From Refugio Grey, head N along the route of Stage 4b. 5min later, TL at the junction at 24. A few minutes later, TR at another junction: follow a clear path N all the way to the fabulous Mirador Grey. After admiring the views, re-trace your steps back to Refugio Grey.

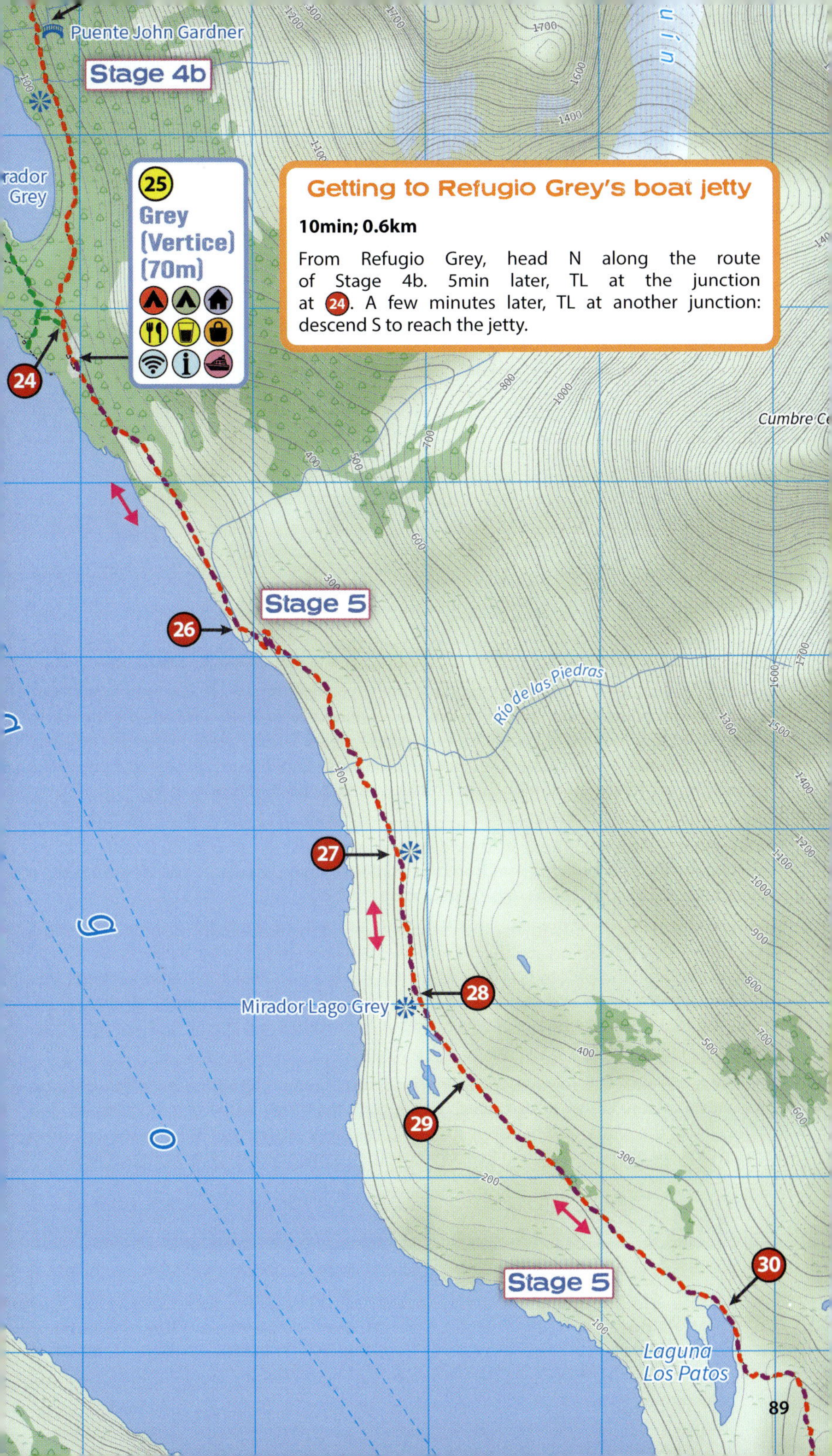
Puente John Gardner
Stage 4b
rador
Grey
25
Grey
(Vertice)
(70m)
24
Getting to Refugio Grey's boat jetty
10min; 0.6km
From Refugio Grey, head N along the route of Stage 4b. 5min later, TL at the junction at 24. A few minutes later, TL at another junction: descend S to reach the jetty.
Cumbre C
Stage 5
26
Río de las Piedras
27
28
Mirador Lago Grey
29
Stage 5
30
Laguna
Los Patos

5 Grey/Paine Grande (O/Q/W)

This gorgeous hike along Lago Grey's E side is shared by OTs, WTs and day-hikers: the trail is therefore busier than the remote N sections of the O. The highest point of the stage is also its mid-point and, in either direction, there is an undulating climb followed by an undulating descent. The N half of the route enjoys fabulous views of Glacier Grey and the stage is best hiked S-N so that you face the glacier all the way down to Refugio Grey: obviously, that is not possible for OTs who are obliged to trek N-S and they will have to remember to look behind regularly to enjoy these views. The icy waters of Lago Grey also look fabulous on this part of the route: usually, there are bright blue icebergs floating in the lake (which can take years to melt after breaking off the snout of Glacier Grey).

For much of the S half of the route, Lago Grey is concealed because the path shifts away from the lake's shoreline. There are, however, fantastic views of Cerro Paine Grande and the Horns (to the E): they look different from this angle compared to the classic view from the S (which you see from the Lago Pehoé Catamaran).

Itinerary options: OTs follow the route N-S and only hike Section 5 in one direction. However, most WTs (starting at either PG or Central) hike Section 5 in both directions, usually overnighting at Refugio/Camping Grey: if you do not want to hike it in both directions, you can start or finish the W at Refugio Grey using the boat between Refugio Grey and HLG to access the trail-head (see p45). For WTs hiking W-E, Section 5 will be the first Section of the trek; for WTs hiking E-W, it is the last Section.

Day-hikers can walk this route too, starting/finishing at either Refugio Grey or PG (because there are boat services at both places). Either walk the stage both ways (arriving at, and leaving from, the same trail-head) or just walk one way (arriving at PG and leaving from Refugio Grey, or vice versa). Day-hikers can also spend the night at PG or Refugio Grey.

	Start	Finish	Time	Distance	Ascent	Descent	Max Alt
5-S	Grey	Paine Grande	3:30	10.8km 6.7miles	319m 1047ft	349m 1145ft	273m 896ft
5-N	Paine Grande	Grey	3:40	10.8km 6.7miles	349m 1145ft	319m 1047ft	273m 896ft

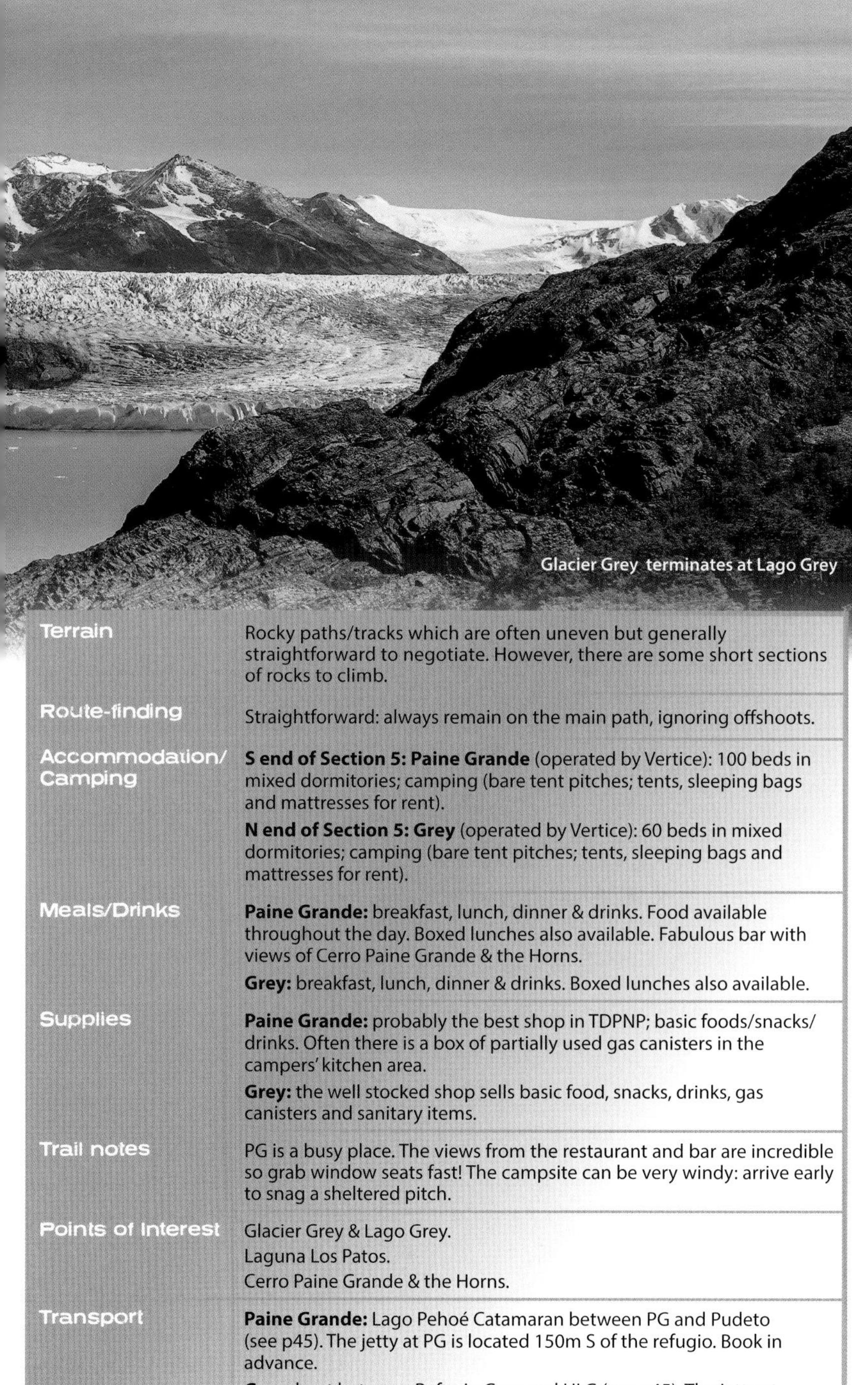

Glacier Grey terminates at Lago Grey

Terrain	Rocky paths/tracks which are often uneven but generally straightforward to negotiate. However, there are some short sections of rocks to climb.
Route-finding	Straightforward: always remain on the main path, ignoring offshoots.
Accommodation/ Camping	**S end of Section 5: Paine Grande** (operated by Vertice): 100 beds in mixed dormitories; camping (bare tent pitches; tents, sleeping bags and mattresses for rent). **N end of Section 5: Grey** (operated by Vertice): 60 beds in mixed dormitories; camping (bare tent pitches; tents, sleeping bags and mattresses for rent).
Meals/Drinks	**Paine Grande:** breakfast, lunch, dinner & drinks. Food available throughout the day. Boxed lunches also available. Fabulous bar with views of Cerro Paine Grande & the Horns. **Grey:** breakfast, lunch, dinner & drinks. Boxed lunches also available.
Supplies	**Paine Grande:** probably the best shop in TDPNP; basic foods/snacks/ drinks. Often there is a box of partially used gas canisters in the campers' kitchen area. **Grey:** the well stocked shop sells basic food, snacks, drinks, gas canisters and sanitary items.
Trail notes	PG is a busy place. The views from the restaurant and bar are incredible so grab window seats fast! The campsite can be very windy: arrive early to snag a sheltered pitch.
Points of Interest	Glacier Grey & Lago Grey. Laguna Los Patos. Cerro Paine Grande & the Horns.
Transport	**Paine Grande:** Lago Pehoé Catamaran between PG and Pudeto (see p45). The jetty at PG is located 150m S of the refugio. Book in advance. **Grey:** boat between Refugio Grey and HLG (see p45). The jetty at Refugio Grey is 0.6km on foot from reception (see p89).

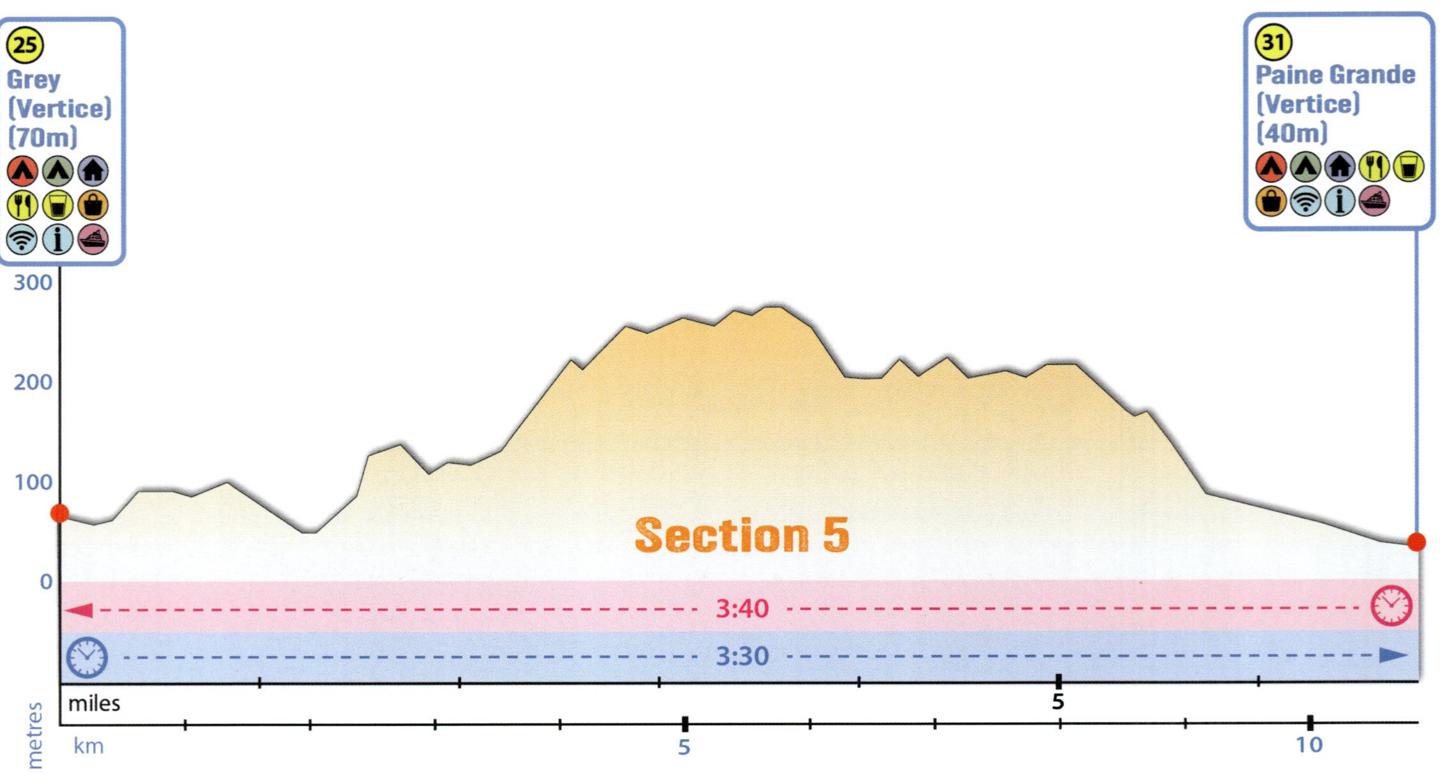

25
Grey
(Vertice)
(70m)
31
Paine Grande
(Vertice)
(40m)
300
200
100
0
metres
Section 5
3:40
3:30
miles
5
km
5
10

Stage 5-S: Grey to Paine Grande

25 See map on p89. From **Refugio Grey**, head S past the restaurant: an undulating path leads S along the slopes above **Lago Grey**. There are some fabulous viewpoints overlooking **Glacier Grey** (to the N).

26 0:40: After descending almost to the shore of the lake, the main climb of the day begins. 10-15min later, pass a spectacular viewpoint. Soon, the path dips briefly and then continues upwards.

27 1:15: Pass another excellent viewpoint.

28 1:45: Reach **Mirador Lago Grey** where you can view both snouts of Glacier Grey.

29 2:05: Cross Section 5's high point. Up until now, the trail has been undulating constantly but gradually gaining height: now the reverse happens and the trail undulates but gradually loses height.

30 2:45: Head around the E side of **Laguna Los Patos** ('Lake of the Ducks'); if there is no wind, the reflections are beautiful. From the lake, the path heads briefly E and then generally SE. See map on p95. Descend through a gorge. As you approach Refugio Paine Grande, **Cerro Paine Grande** and **the Horns** are visible to the E. Pass to the left of the **ranger station**.

31 3:30: Shortly afterwards, reach **Refugio/Camping Paine Grande (40m)**.

Stage 5-N: Paine Grande to Grey

31 See map on p95. From **Refugio Paine Grande**, head NE and pass to the right of the **ranger station**. Afterwards, TL and head NW. Climb through a gorge.

30 1:10: See map on p89. Head around the E side of **Laguna Los Patos** ('Lake of the Ducks'): if there is no wind, the reflections are beautiful.

29 2:00: Cross Section 5's high point. Up until now, the trail has been undulating constantly but gradually gaining height: now the reverse happens and the trail undulates but gradually loses height.

28 2:20: Reach **Mirador Lago Grey** where you can view both snouts of **Glacier Grey**.

27 2:40: Pass another excellent viewpoint.

26 3:00: Descend almost to the shore of the lake. Then continue N (initially climbing).

25 3:40: Reach **Refugio/Camping Grey (70m)**.

Lago Grey at sunrise

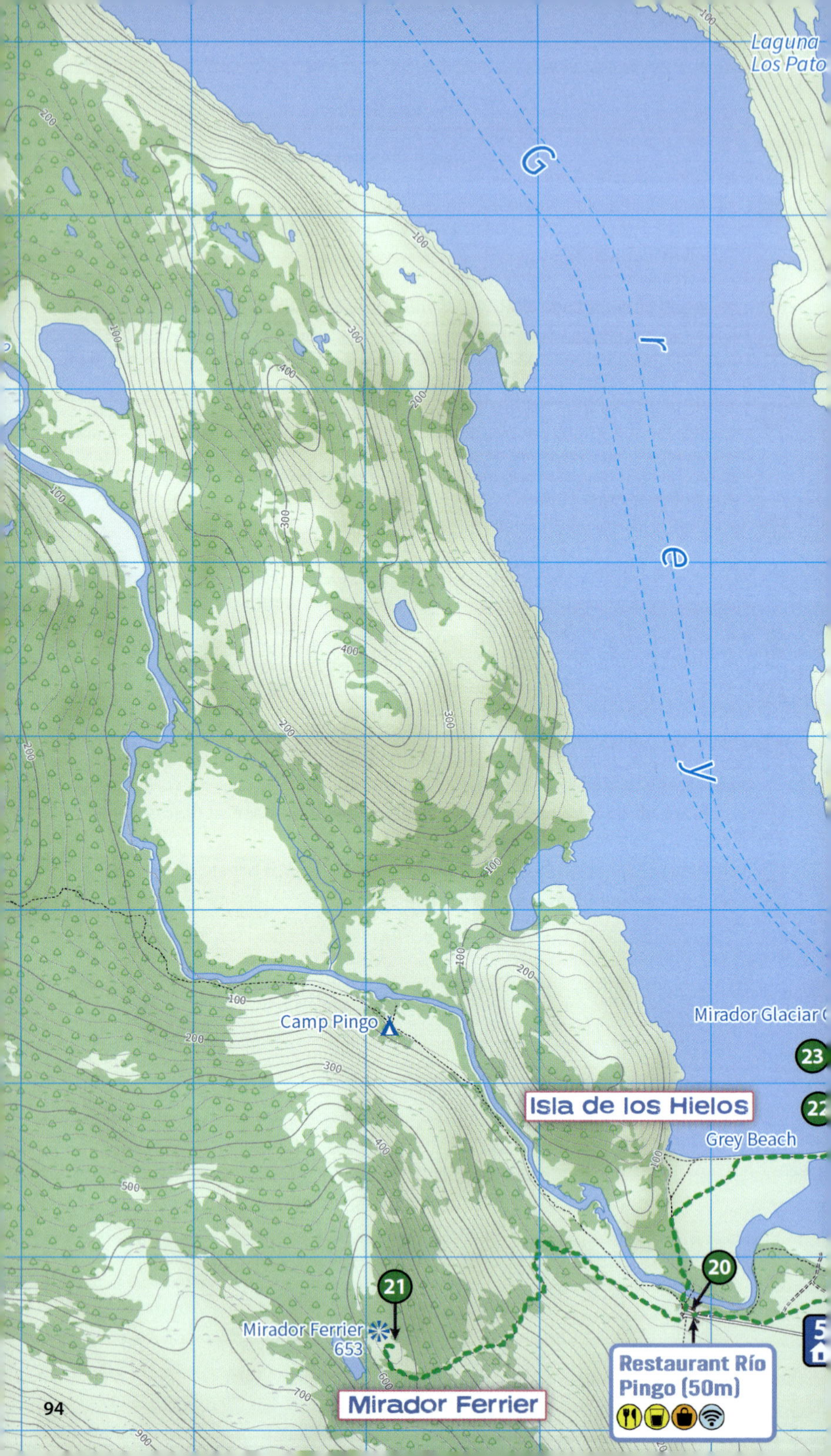
Laguna
Los Pato
G
r
e
y
Camp Pingo
Mirador Glaciar
23
Isla de los Hielos
22
Grey Beach
20
21
Mirador Ferrier
653
Mirador Ferrier
Restaurant Río
Pingo (50m)
5

Stage 6a
Stage 5
Lago
31
Paine Grande (Vertice) (40m)
32
8
9
The Q Extension
Lago
Mirador Pehoé
Lago Grey Jetty
Hotel Lago Grey (50m)
Río Grey

6 Paine Grande/Francés, via Mirador Británico (O/Q/W)

Section 6 is a clear highlight of both the O and the W. Stage 6a's journey along the W side of turquoise Lago Skottsberg is fabulous, passing underneath Cerro Paine Grande and providing superb views of the Horns. However, Stage 6b's climb (and descent) of Valle del Francés is nothing short of sublime on a clear day: all the way up the valley, the path overlooks Glacier del Francés and it is a humbling experience to witness enormous chunks of ice breaking off the glacier and crashing down into the valley. The climb culminates at Mirador Británico which is located within a huge cirque at the top of the valley. The 360° panorama on display there is extraordinary: you find yourself directly below the Horns to the E; to the W is Cerro Paine Grande; and to the N, you can see Cerro Cathedral, Cerro Castillo and a host of other peaks.

When hiked in full, Section 6 is a very long day and is one of the toughest stages of the O/W: 21.5km in one day (with significant altitude gain/loss) may be too much for less fit trekkers. Consequently, some people skip all or part of Stage 6b, either by design at planning stage or because they discover on the trail that they are too tired to undertake it. Hikers may also skip it because they are short of time or the weather is bad.

Some trekkers maintain that Section 6 is best hiked W-E because the finest scenery is saved until the latter parts of the day, with Stage 6a serving as a scenic (and physical) warm-up for the marvellous (and tougher) Stage 6b. However, others prefer to hike E-W, undertaking the toughest section (Valle del Francés) at the start of the day rather than leaving it to the end.

Itinerary options: although you pass Campamento Italiano mid-section, camping is not currently permitted there and accordingly, you can no longer use it to split Section 6. However, there is another way to divide the Section and hike it over two days (although it requires some backtracking): see p25 (W-E) or p31 (E-W).

Trekkers planning to skip Stage 6b could hike between Refugio Grey and Refugio Francés in one day, or between PG and Cuernos.

	Start	Finish	Time	Distance	Ascent (W-E)	Descent (W-E)	Max Alt
6a	Paine Grande	Italiano	2:30 2:15	7.7km 4.8miles	219m 719ft	99m 325ft	170m 558ft
6b	Italiano	Italiano	4:40 4:40	12.8km 8.0miles	615m 2018ft	615m 2018ft	770m 2526ft
6c	Italiano	Francés	0:20 0:20	1.0km 0.6miles	37m 121ft	22m 72ft	180m 591ft

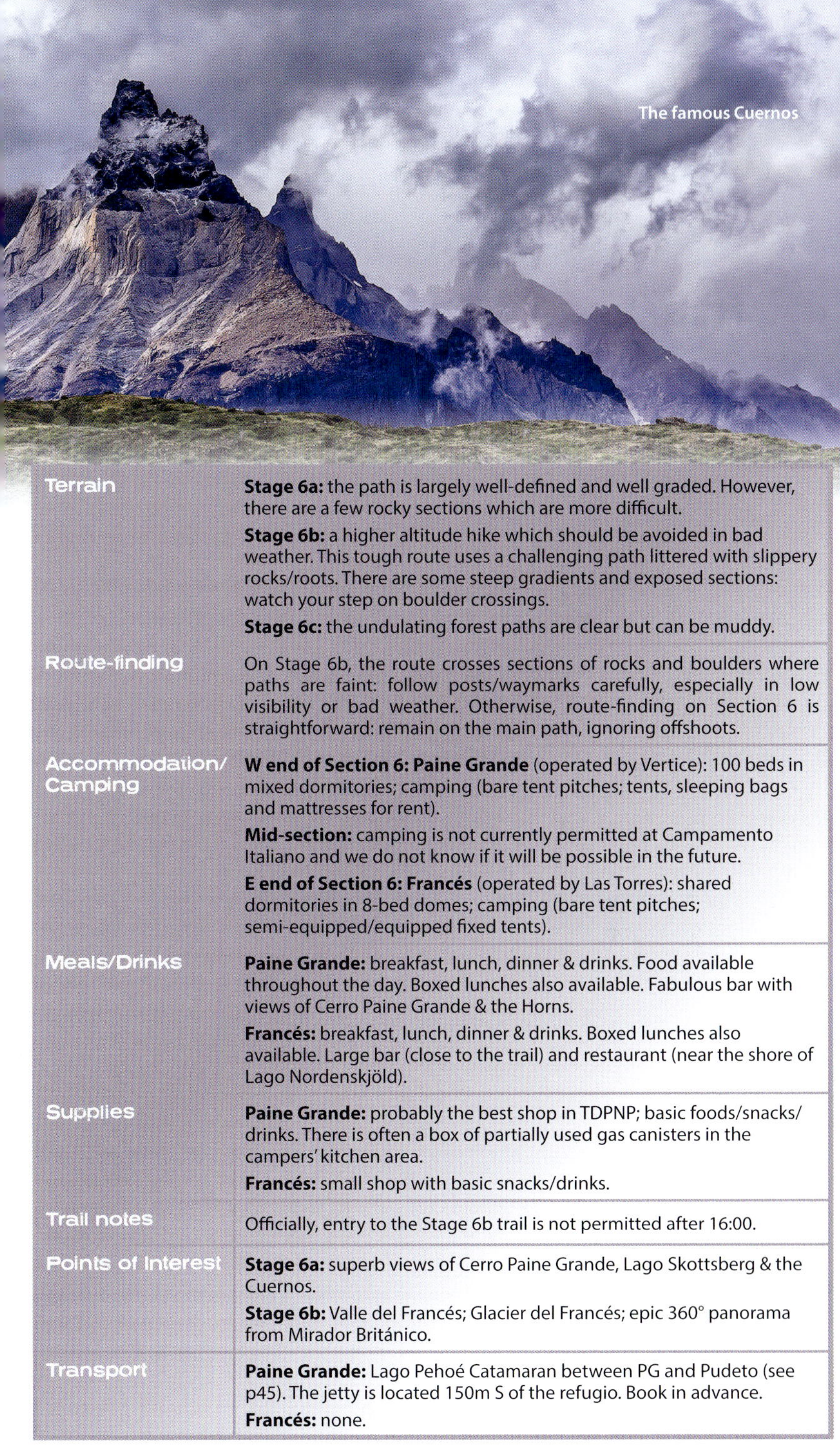
The famous Cuernos

Terrain	**Stage 6a:** the path is largely well-defined and well graded. However, there are a few rocky sections which are more difficult. **Stage 6b:** a higher altitude hike which should be avoided in bad weather. This tough route uses a challenging path littered with slippery rocks/roots. There are some steep gradients and exposed sections: watch your step on boulder crossings. **Stage 6c:** the undulating forest paths are clear but can be muddy.
Route-finding	On Stage 6b, the route crosses sections of rocks and boulders where paths are faint: follow posts/waymarks carefully, especially in low visibility or bad weather. Otherwise, route-finding on Section 6 is straightforward: remain on the main path, ignoring offshoots.
Accommodation/ Camping	**W end of Section 6: Paine Grande** (operated by Vertice): 100 beds in mixed dormitories; camping (bare tent pitches; tents, sleeping bags and mattresses for rent). **Mid-section:** camping is not currently permitted at Campamento Italiano and we do not know if it will be possible in the future. **E end of Section 6: Francés** (operated by Las Torres): shared dormitories in 8-bed domes; camping (bare tent pitches; semi-equipped/equipped fixed tents).
Meals/Drinks	**Paine Grande:** breakfast, lunch, dinner & drinks. Food available throughout the day. Boxed lunches also available. Fabulous bar with views of Cerro Paine Grande & the Horns. **Francés:** breakfast, lunch, dinner & drinks. Boxed lunches also available. Large bar (close to the trail) and restaurant (near the shore of Lago Nordenskjöld).
Supplies	**Paine Grande:** probably the best shop in TDPNP; basic foods/snacks/ drinks. There is often a box of partially used gas canisters in the campers' kitchen area. **Francés:** small shop with basic snacks/drinks.
Trail notes	Officially, entry to the Stage 6b trail is not permitted after 16:00.
Points of Interest	**Stage 6a:** superb views of Cerro Paine Grande, Lago Skottsberg & the Cuernos. **Stage 6b:** Valle del Francés; Glacier del Francés; epic 360° panorama from Mirador Británico.
Transport	**Paine Grande:** Lago Pehoé Catamaran between PG and Pudeto (see p45). The jetty is located 150m S of the refugio. Book in advance. **Francés:** none.

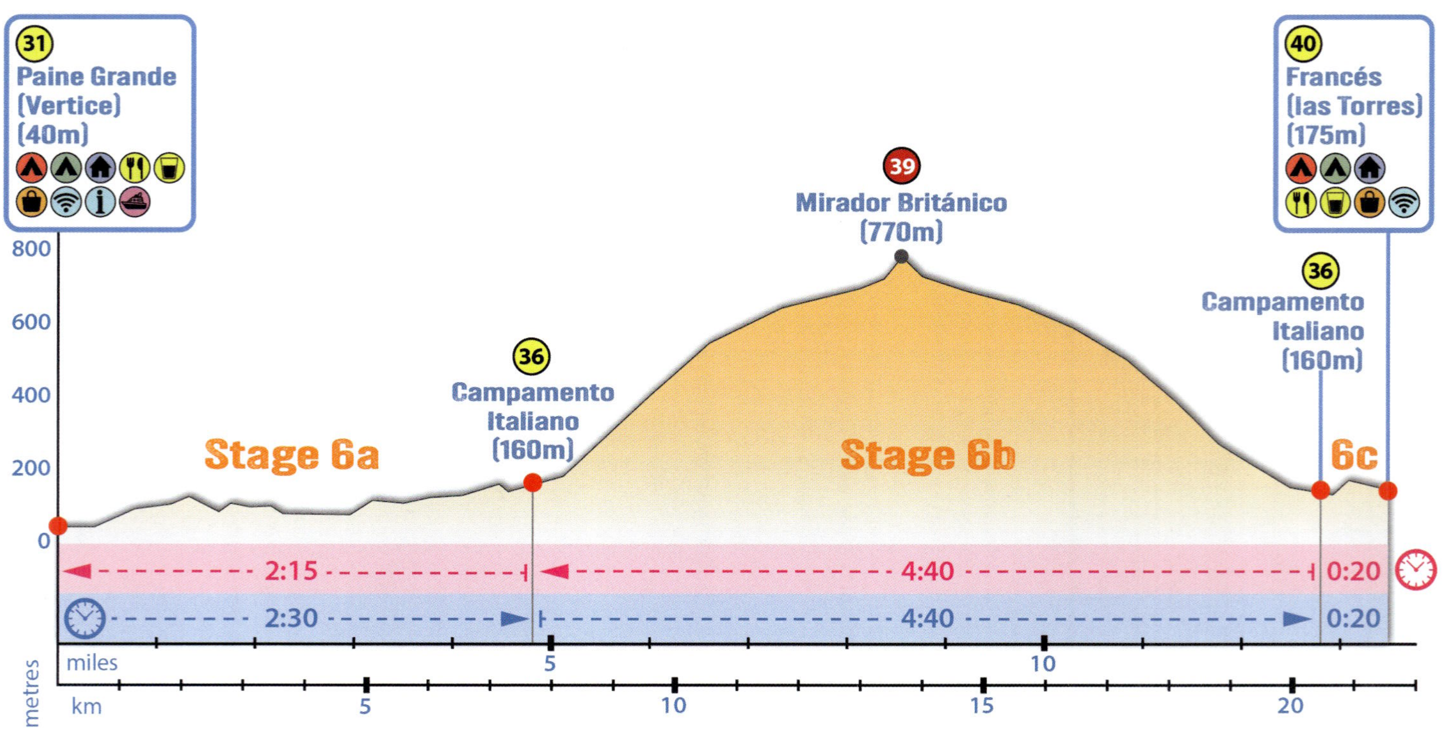

31
Paine Grande (Vertice) (40m)
36
Campamento Italiano (160m)
39
Mirador Británico (770m)
36
Campamento Italiano (160m)
40
Francés (las Torres) (175m)
Stage 6a
Stage 6b
6c
800
600
400
200
0
metres
2:15
4:40
0:20
2:30
4:40
0:20
miles
5
10
km
5
10
15
20

Stage 6a (W-E): Paine Grande to Italiano

31 **See map on p95.** From **Refugio Paine Grande**, head NE and pass to the right of the ranger station. Afterwards, keep SH (heading E).

32 0:15: TL at a junction; alternatively, TR for a variant path which heads around the E side of **Lago Skottsberg**. Afterwards, there are some excellent viewpoints.

33 1:05: **See map on p100.** Pass a superb viewpoint over **Lago Skottsberg**. Later, walk along a board-walk: magnificent views of **the Horns**.

34 1:45: Just after exiting the board-walk, cross a stream.

35 2:15: Keep SH at a junction (the variant route around Lago Skottsberg rejoins from the right). Immediately afterwards, cross a suspension bridge.

36 2:30: Reach the junction at **Campamento Italiano (160m)**.

Stage 6b (W-E): Italiano to Italiano (Valle del Francés side-trip)

36 **See map on p101.** From the junction, head N. Shortly afterwards, reach the ranger station at **Campamento Italiano**: you can leave your pack here while you hike up Valle del Francés. Climb N on a rough path up the E side of the valley.

37 0:40: Cross a long section of boulders (red posts and waymarks). The views of **Glacier Francés** are amazing.

38 1:30: Pass **Mirador Valle del Francis**. Afterwards, continue up the valley. Later, the path undulates tiringly along steep rocky banks. When you emerge from the trees, cross a broad rocky plateau with 360° views. Afterwards, enter trees again and continue steeply upwards.

39 2:55: Reach the spectacular **Mirador Británico (770m)**. After admiring the views, retrace your steps.

36 4:40: Pass the ranger station to reach the junction at **Campamento Italiano (160m)**.

Stage 6c (W-E): Italiano to Francés

36 **See map on p101.** From the junction, head E. The path undulates through trees.

40 0:20: Arrive at **Refugio/Camping Francés (175m)**.

Stage 6c (E-W): Francés to Italiano

40 **See map on p101.** From **Refugio Francés**, the path undulates W through trees.

36 0:20: Reach the junction at **Campamento Italiano (160m)**. TL for PG (Stage 6a) or keep SH for Valle del Francés (Stage 6b).

Stage 6b (E-W): Italiano to Italiano (Valle del Francés side-trip)

See W-E directions above.

Stage 6a (E-W): Italiano to Paine Grande

36 **See map on p101.** From the junction at **Campamento Italiano**, head initially S ('Paine Grande').

35 0:10: Cross a suspension bridge. Immediately afterwards, TR at a junction: alternatively, TL for a variant path which heads around the E side of **Lago Skottsberg**.

34 0:35: Cross a stream. Just afterwards, walk along a board-walk: behind there are magnificent views of **the Horns**.

33 1:15: Pass a superb viewpoint over **Lago Skottsberg** with **the Horns** in the background. Later on, there are more excellent viewpoints.

32 2:00: **See map on p95.** Keep SH at a junction (the variant route rejoins on the left).

31 2:15: Just after passing to the left of the ranger station, reach **Refugio/Camping Paine Grande (40m)**.

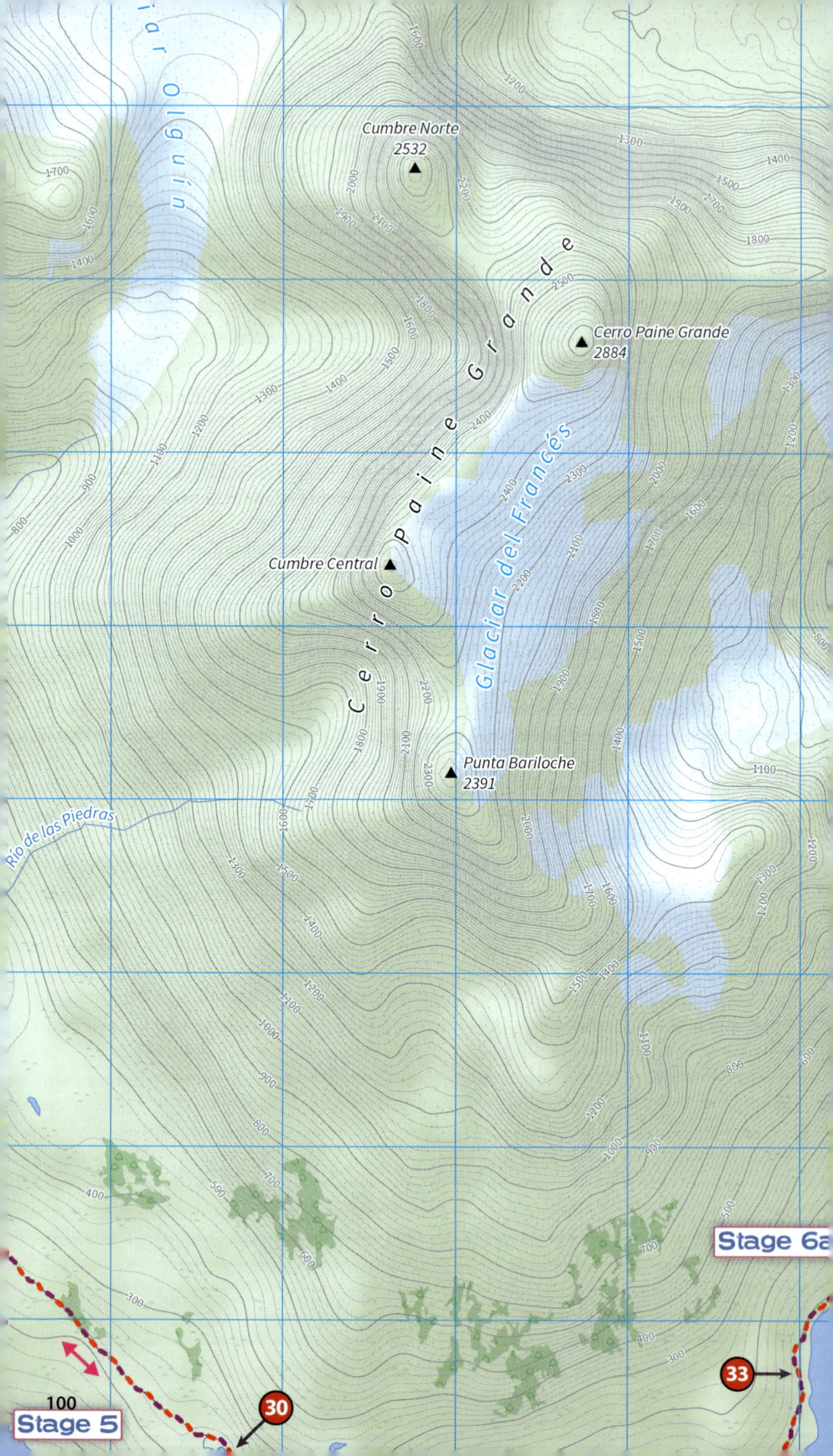

Cumbre Norte
2532
Cerro Paine Grande
Cerro Paine Grande
2884
Glaciar del Francés
Cumbre Central
Punta Bariloche
2391
Río de las Piedras
Stage 6a
Stage 5
30
33
100

Mirador Británico 770m
Valle del Francés
Mirador Ouairy
Cuerno Norte
2168
Cuernos del Paine
Cuerno Principal
2251
2200
Stage 6b
Valle del Francés
Río del Francés
Mirador del Glaciar Francés
40
Francés (las Torres) (175m)
Stage 7a
Campamento Italiano
160m
6c
Stage 6a
34
35
36
37
38
39
15
Mirador Cuernos
Salto Gr

7 Francés/Chileno (O/Q/W)

This magnificent hike along the N shore of the bright turquoise Lago Nordenskjöld can be divided into three parts. Firstly, the W section passes through the forest below the Horns as it travels between Refugio Francés and Refugio Cuernos. The middle part, however, takes advantage of more open slopes to deliver exquisite views of the lake, the Horns and many other peaks: this section is extremely beautiful but it is also tiring because the path undulates regularly. Lastly, the E section leads you across more elevated slopes (further above the lake) and with the increased altitude comes even better lake views: this part of the route is harder for W-E trekkers who climb all the way from 45 to the exposed Windy Pass.

Itinerary options: fit trekkers could hike the return trip to Mirador TDP (Stage 8a) on the same day as hiking between Francés and Chileno: this is easier for E-W trekkers because Stage 7b has less climbing in that direction; however, for W-E trekkers, this is a very tough day. Extremely fit trekkers, could even descend from Chileno to Central on the same day.

OTs and WTs travelling W-E who cannot get a booking at Chileno could instead hike from Refugio Francés to Central using the Cuernos-Central Direct Route (see p118): the following morning, after a night at Central, you would climb to Mirador TDP and back (Stages 8b/8a/8b). For further information, see p110.

Private cabins at Cuernos

	Start	Finish	Time	Distance	Ascent (W-E)	Descent (W-E)	Max Alt
7a	Francés	Cuernos	1:00 1:10	3.5km 2.2miles	58m 190ft	148m 486ft	215m 705ft
7b	Cuernos	Chileno	4:15 3:35	12.2km 7.6miles	613m 2011ft	288m 945ft	471m 1545ft

Lago Nordenskjöld

Terrain	**Stage 7a:** undulating forest paths which can be muddy; slippery rocks/roots. **Stage 7b:** the path is largely clear and well graded. However, there are some rocky sections which are more difficult. Between (42) and (45) the route undulates significantly and is more tiring than it appears on the map. Between (45) and (48), the path climbs although gradients are rarely very steep. As its name suggests, Windy Pass (48) is an exposed and windy place: avoid it in bad weather or very high winds.
Route-finding	The route between (45) and (46) is a little unclear. Otherwise, route-finding is straightforward.
Accommodation/ Camping	**W end of Section 6: Francés** (operated by Las Torres): shared dormitories in 8-bed domes; camping (bare tent pitches; semi-equipped/equipped fixed tents). **Mid-Section: Cuernos**: (operated by Las Torres): 6-bed dormitories; 8 private mountain cabins (2-3 people in each); camping (bare tent pitches; semi-equipped/equipped fixed tents). **E end of Section 7: Chileno** (operated by Las Torres): camping only (bare tent pitches; semi-equipped/equipped fixed tents).
Meals/Drinks	**Francés:** breakfast, lunch, dinner & drinks. Boxed lunches also available. Large bar (close to the trail) and restaurant (near the shore of Lago Nordenskjöld). **Cuernos:** breakfast, lunch, dinner & drinks. Boxed lunches available. **Chileno:** breakfast, lunch, dinner & drinks. Boxed lunches available.
Supplies	**Francés:** basic snacks/drinks. **Cuernos:** basic snacks/drinks. **Chileno:** basic snacks/drinks.
Trail notes	Chileno can be a damp and windy place. The use of camping stoves is prohibited at Chileno.
Points of Interest	**Stage 7a:** Lago Nordenskjöld. **Stage 7b:** fabulous views of the Horns, Punta Bariloche, Cima Central and Lago Nordenskjöld; Windy Pass.
Transport	None.

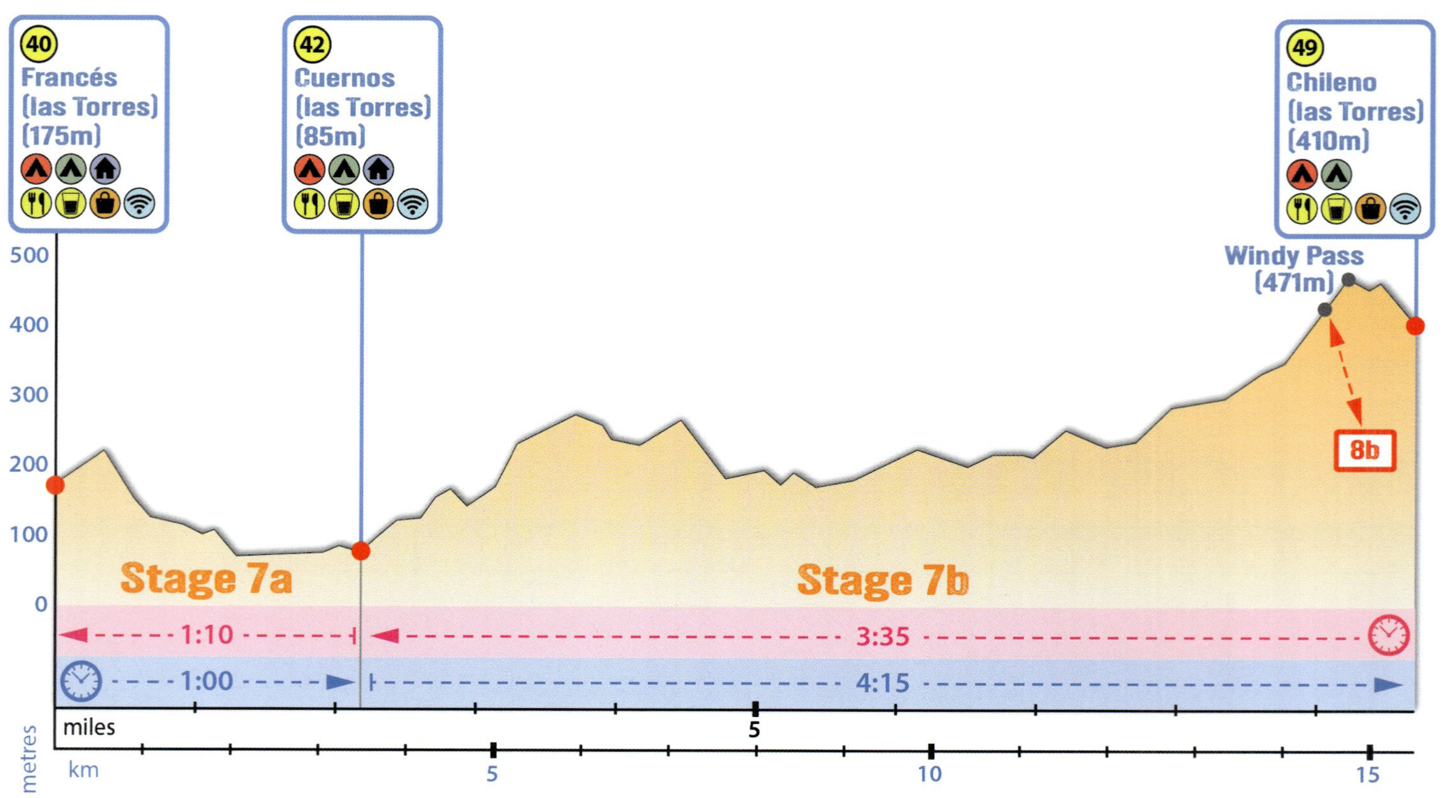
40
Francés
(las Torres)
(175m)
42
Cuernos
(las Torres)
(85m)
49
Chileno
(las Torres)
(410m)
Windy Pass
(471m)
8b
500
400
300
200
100
0
metres
Stage 7a
Stage 7b
1:10
3:35
1:00
4:15
miles
5
km
5
10
15

Stage 7a (W-E): Francés to Cuernos

40 See map on p106. From **Refugio Francés**, climb E through the forest. After 10min, the path starts to descend. When you reach **Lago Nordenskjöld**, head E along the rocky shore.

41 0:40: Cross a stream on rocks.

42 1:00: Arrive at **Refugio/Camping Cuernos (85m)**.

Stage 7b (W-E): Cuernos to Chileno

42 See map on p106. From **Refugio Cuernos**, head E. The path now contours around the slopes towards **the Horns**: behind, you can see **Punta Bariloche** and **Cima Central**.

43 1:10: Pass **Mirador Cuernos**, an incredible viewpoint, overlooking Lago Nordenskjöld.

44 1:35: Cross a suspension bridge over a torrent.

45 2:30: TL at a junction ('Short-cut to Chileno').

46 2:35: Cross a stream. Immediately afterwards, climb the stream bank and then TL to climb NE on a path.

47 2:50: See map on p109. Cross a stream on rocks. A magnificent path climbs gently N away from the lake: contour around the slopes (which are dotted with Chilean firebush).

48 4:00: TL at a junction. Shortly afterwards, cross **Windy Pass (471m)** and descend NW on a rocky path.

49 4:15: Cross a bridge over **Río Ascencio** to arrive at **Camping Chileno (410m)**.

Stage 7b (E-W): Chileno to Cuernos

49 See map on p109. From **Camping Chileno**, head S and cross a bridge over **Río Ascencio**. Climb S on the rocky path and cross **Windy Pass (471m)**: afterwards, start to descend.

48 0:30: Shortly afterwards, TR at a junction. The magnificent path descends S towards **Lago Nordenskjöld**, gently contouring around the slopes (which are dotted with Chilean firebush).

47 1:05: Cross a stream on rocks.

46 1:20: At a faint junction above a stream, descend to the right. Then cross the stream and pick up a path on the other side.

45 1:25: TR at a junction and head SW.

44 2:20: See map on p107. Cross a suspension bridge over a torrent.

43 2:45: Pass **Mirador Cuernos**, an incredible viewpoint overlooking Lago Nordenskjöld; you can see **the Cuernos** to the NW. The path now contours around the slopes towards the Cuernos. Soon **Punta Bariloche** and **Cima Central** appear to the left of the Cuernos.

42 3:35: Shortly after crossing a bridge, reach **Refugio/Camping Cuernos (85m)**.

Stage 7a (E-W): Cuernos to Francés

42 See map on p106. From **Refugio Cuernos**, head W through trees. Descend all the way to the shore of **Lago Nordenskjöld**. There are superb views of **Cerro Paine Grande**.

41 0:20: Cross a stream on rocks. 5min later, walk along the rocky shore of the lake. Soon, the path heads back inland and climbs.

40 1:10: Arrive at **Refugio/Camping Francés (175m)**.

Cerro Espada
Británico 770m
Valle Bader
Ouairy
Cuerno Norte
2168
Cuernos del Paine
Cuerno Principal
2251
Cuerno Este
2200
Río Bader
37
40
Francés
(las Torres)
(175m)
42
Cuernos
(las Torres)
(85m)
Stage 7a
36
6c
41
35
Lago

Monte Almirante Nieto
2640
Stage
47
46
45
7
Stage 7b
Río del Arriero
44
Mirador Cuernos
43
Stage 7b
N o r d e n s k j ö
Mirador Nordenskjöld
07
P

Cerro Nido de Cóndor
2243
Torre Norte
2260
Torre Central
2460
Torre Sur
2501
Torres del Paine
Mirador Torres del Paine
900
Lago Torres
Guardería Torres
51
50
Valle As
Monte Almirante Nieto
2640
Stage 7

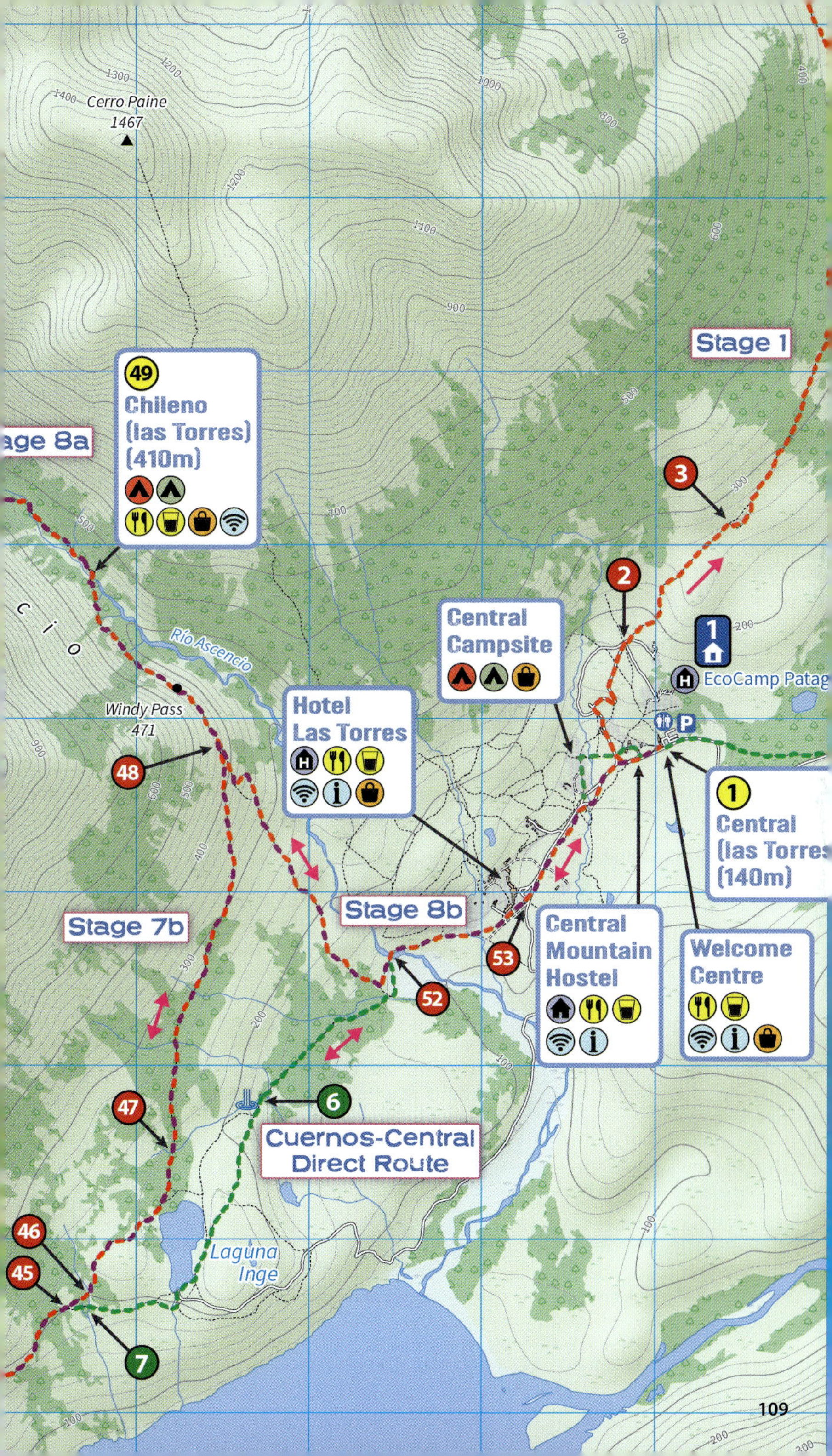

Cerro Paine
1467
Stage 1
49
Chileno
(las Torres)
(410m)
age 8a
Río Ascencio
Windy Pass
471
Central
Campsite
Hotel
Las Torres
EcoCamp Patag
1
Central
(las Torres
(140m)
Stage 8b
Stage 7b
Central
Mountain
Hostel
Welcome
Centre
Cuernos-Central
Direct Route
Laguna
Inge

Chileno/Central, via Mirador Torres del Paine (O/Q/W)

If you are lucky enough to visit it on a fine day, Mirador Torres del Paine may be the overall highlight of your trek. The Towers of Paine are three impressive pointed towers (Torre Norte, Torre Central and Torre Sur), perched on a snow-capped ridge high above the strikingly bright Lago Torres. The view from the mirador is one of the classic images of TDPNP. The unusual shape of the Towers is exceptionally dramatic and the vibrant turquoise colour of the lake, when lit up by the sun, has to be seen to be believed: if the sun does show up, take your pictures fast as it can very quickly disappear again.

After spending the night at Chileno and climbing to Mirador TDP the following morning, OTs and WTs travelling W-E simply return to Chileno and then descend along Stage 8b to Central to finish the hike and catch the bus out of TDPNP. However, WTs travelling E-W have a few different options. Many E-W trekkers climb to Chileno on the day of arrival in TDPNP and spend the night there. The following day, they climb to Mirador TDP: fit trekkers can continue to the subsequent accommodation at Refugio Cuernos (using Stage 7b) that same day. However, for some, the hike from Chileno to Mirador TDP and back will be enough for one day and they will not want to contemplate an additional 12km to reach Cuernos. The solution is to plan a second night at Chileno or Central to rest up before hiking to Cuernos/ Francés the following day: if your second night is at Chileno, you will use Stage 7b to reach Cuernos the following day; on the other hand, if your second night is at Central, you can use the Cuernos-Central Direct Route the following day (p118). Very fit WTs travelling E-W could even hike Central-Mirador TDP-Cuernos, all on the same day.

It is also possible for both OTs and WTs starting at Central to hike to Mirador TDP on the day of arrival in the park. You would need to take an early bus to TDPNP and move fast: you would visit the Mirador in the afternoon and should take heed of the trail closure times (see p111). If you intend to do this, it is best to spend your first night at Chileno. However, if you cannot get a booking at Chileno, it is possible to climb from Central all the way to Mirador TDP and back again, all in one very long day: this may be too much for inexperienced trekkers.

An afternoon trip to Mirador TDP can be spectacular because the sun amplifies the incredible colour of Lago Torres. However, the best time to visit it is probably sunrise, when the rising sun paints the granite towers a vivid shade of red. To reach the viewpoint before sunrise, you have to start the hike well before dawn. For this reason, it is best for sunrise hikers to spend the night at Chileno and start the climb from there early the following morning (skipping breakfast): sunrise hikers starting the climb from Central will have to get up even earlier. Before you decide to get up so early, bear in mind that the weather in TDP is notoriously capricious and that the Towers only light up if there are no clouds blocking the sun's rays: although there is a chance that you could enjoy some of the best views of your life, bad weather could leave you disappointed so it is wise to manage your expectations. If you are starting your trek from Central and planning a sunrise hike to Mirador TDP, then there is no need to get the earliest bus from PN to TDPNP: however, it is not a bad idea to do so anyway because, if the skies are clear when you arrive, then you could hike up to Mirador TDP straight away to take advantage of the good weather; if you still had energy, you could go up a second time for sunrise the following morning or stay in bed longer instead.

OTs starting at Central can actually factor in two shots at the Towers: one at the start of the trek and one at the end. On the day of arrival, climb from Central to Mirador TDP and return to Central to spend your first night: the following day, hike Section 1 of the O. If the weather was bad and you did not see much of the Towers, then you still have another shot at the end of your O circuit. Even if you are not starting at Central, you can plan two consecutive nights at Central to allow for two attempts on the Towers: if you were exceptionally lucky with the weather, you could witness it both at sunrise and later in the day.

	Start	Finish	Time	Distance	Ascent (W-E)	Descent (W-E)	Max Alt
8a	Chileno	Chileno	3:45 3:45	9.6km 6.0miles	490m 1608ft	490m 1608ft	900m 2953ft
8b	Chileno	Central	1:35 2:15	5.5km 3.4miles	110m 361ft	380m 1247ft	471m 1545ft

Terrain	**Stage 8a:** a high altitude hike which should be avoided in bad weather. Much of the route lies within forest: paths are largely well-defined but they can be muddy (with slippery rocks/roots). However, between (50) and (51), a more challenging path rises above the tree-line: steep gradients; slippery rocks/roots; sections of boulders to cross. **Stage 8b:** the path is largely clear and well graded. However, there are a few rocky sections which are more difficult. Between (48) and (52), the gradient can be steep and the surface is sometimes loose and unstable. As its name suggests, Windy Pass is a windy and exposed place: avoid it in bad weather/high winds.
Route-finding	**Stage 8a:** between (50) and (51), the route crosses sections of rocks and boulders where paths are faint: follow signs and orange posts carefully, especially in low visibility/bad weather. Otherwise, route-finding is straightforward: remain on the main path, ignoring offshoots. **Stage 8b:** between (48) and (52), the path splinters but branches usually converge. Otherwise, route-finding is straightforward (signs/orange posts).
Accommodation/ Camping	**Chileno** (operated by Las Torres)**:** camping only (bare tent pitches; semi-equipped/equipped fixed tents). **Central** (everything operated by Las Torres)**:** ▶ **Central Mountain Hostel:** mixed 6-bed dormitories. ▶ **Central Campsite:** bare tent pitches; semi-equipped/equipped fixed tents. ▶ **Hotel Las Torres:** luxurious private rooms.
Meals/Drinks	**Chileno:** breakfast, lunch, dinner & drinks. Boxed lunches available. **Central Welcome Centre:** café (drinks/snacks). **Central Mountain Hostel:** breakfast, lunch, dinner & drinks; snacks throughout the day. Boxed lunches also available. Food is available to those staying at either the hostel or the campsite. **Hotel Las Torres:** breakfast, lunch, dinner & drinks; snacks during the day.
Supplies	**Chileno:** basic snacks/drinks. **Central Welcome Centre:** basic food, snacks and outdoor gear. **Central Campsite:** basic snacks. **Hotel Las Torres:** snacks and possibly some basic outdoor gear.
Trail notes	Entry to the trails is prohibited after certain times: ▶ **Refugio Chileno (49) to Guardería Torres (50):** no entry after 14:00. ▶ **Guardería Torres (50) to Mirador TDP (51):** no entry after 15:00. ▶ **Mirador TDP (51):** closes 16:00. Central is a fragmented and confusing place. The shuttle bus drops off and picks up at the car park beside the Welcome Centre.
Points of Interest	Superlative views of the Towers. This is one of the busiest trails in TDPNP. To avoid the crowds, start the climb to Mirador TDP in the morning (the earlier the better).
Transport	**Central:** shuttle bus to Laguna Amarga.

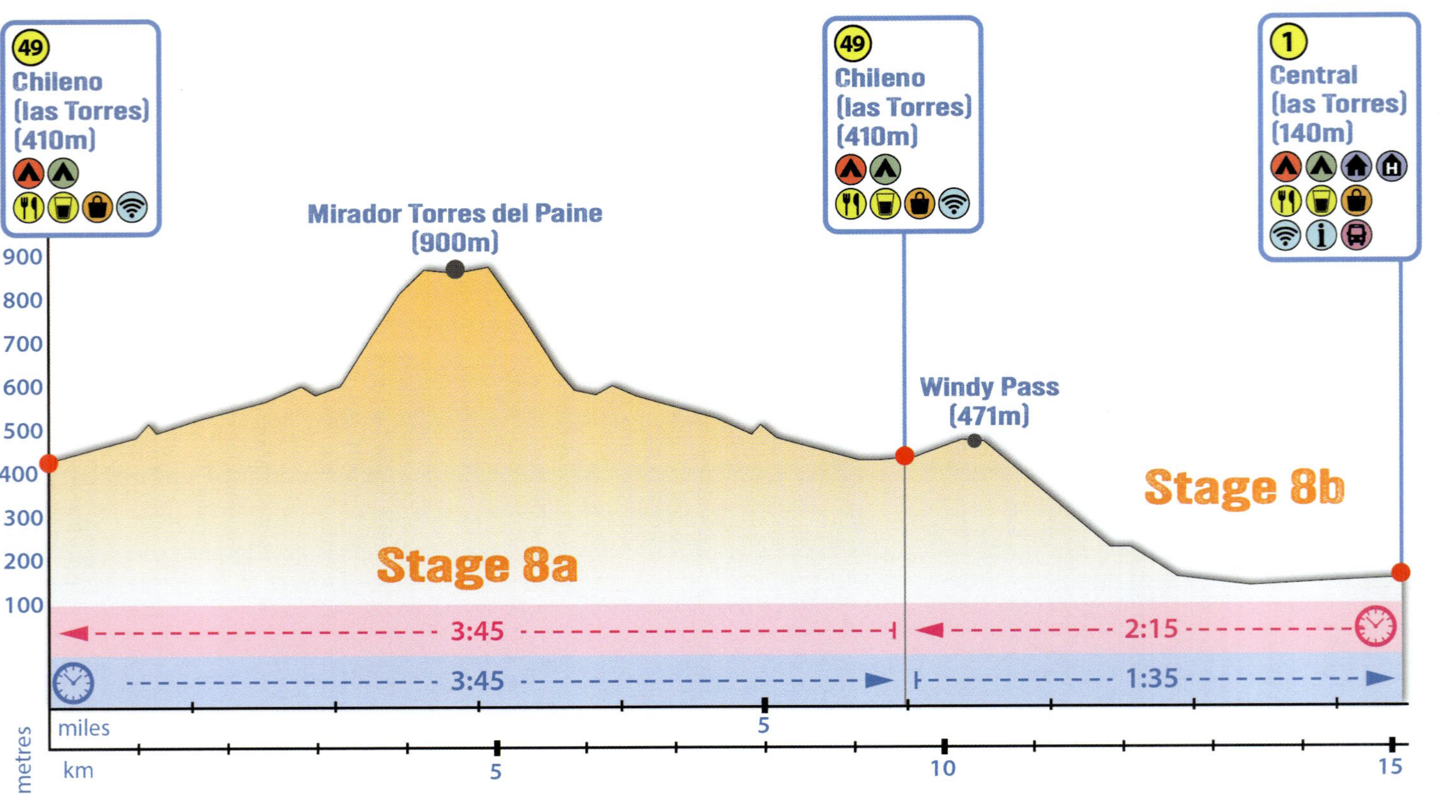
49
Chileno
(las Torres)
(410m)
Mirador Torres del Paine
(900m)
49
Chileno
(las Torres)
(410m)
Windy Pass
(471m)
1
Central
(las Torres)
(140m)
900
800
700
600
500
400
300
200
100
metres
Stage 8a
Stage 8b
3:45
3:45
2:15
1:35
miles
5
km
5
10
15

Mirador Torres del Paine

Packhorses approaching Windy Pass

Stage 8a (W-E): Chileno to Chileno (via Mirador TDP)

(49) See map on p109. From **Camping Chileno**, head NW ('Las Torres'). After 10min, cross a bridge over the river. Then climb through trees. Soon, cross another bridge and continue through the forest.

(50) 1:05: Pass **Guardería Torres** (toilet). Afterwards, the path climbs steeply W through trees. When you emerge from the trees, the path climbs through boulders. Bear right at a viewpoint of the Towers and take care hopping across boulders. Finally, the undulating route bends left: climb towards the Towers.

(51) 2:15: Reach **Mirador Torres del Paine (900m)**. From there, you can continue down to the edge of **Lago Torres**. Afterwards, retrace your steps back towards Chileno.

(49) 3:45: Arrive at **Camping Chileno (410m)**.

Stage 8b (W-E): Chileno to Central

(49) See map on p109. From **Camping Chileno**, head S and cross a bridge over **Río Ascencio**. Climb S on the rocky path previously travelled on Stage 7b. Cross **Windy Pass (471m)** and start to descend.

(48) 0:30: Shortly afterwards, TL at a junction and descend SE on a path (which occasionally splinters): remain on the main path, following orange posts.

(52) 1:05: Keep SH at a junction and cross a suspension bridge. Then follow the path E.

(53) 1:20: At **Hotel Las Torres** (a sprawling group of buildings with a beautiful location on a grassy plain beneath **Cerro Paine**), keep SH at a junction. Just afterwards, pick up a path which runs parallel to a track (on its S side): continue NE. The path meets the track again at a junction: continue NE on the track to head to the Welcome Centre; alternatively, head N for **Central Campsite**. Continuing NE, after 5min, a path on the left heads to **Central Mountain Hostel**: keep SH on the track for the Welcome Centre.

(1) 1:35: Reach the **Welcome Centre** at **Central (140m)**.

Stage 8b (E-W): Central to Chileno

1 See map on p109. From the **Welcome Centre**, head WSW on a path. A few minutes later, keep SH at a junction: alternatively, TR for **Central Mountain Hostel**. Shortly afterwards, head W on a track. Shortly after that, keep SH at a junction: alternatively, TR on a track for **Central Campsite** or **Serón**. Continue SW on the track or pick up a path which runs parallel to the track (on its S side).

53 0:15: TR at a fork and walk SW past **Hotel Las Torres**, a sprawling group of buildings with a beautiful location on a grassy plain beneath **Cerro Paine**.

52 0:30: Cross a suspension bridge. Immediately afterwards, TR at a junction and climb on a path (which occasionally splinters): remain on the main path, following orange posts.

48 2:00: Keep SH at a junction: the path on the left heads to Refugio Cuernos (Stage 7b). Shortly afterwards, cross **Windy Pass (471m)** and descend NW on a rocky path.

49 2:15: Cross a bridge over **Río Ascencio** to arrive at **Camping Chileno (410m)**.

Stage 8a (E-W): Chileno to Chileno (via Mirador TDP)

See Stage 8a (W-E) on p114.

Equipped tents at Chileno

0 Walk-in/out: Laguna Amarga/ Central

Instead of taking the Las Torres shuttle bus between Laguna Amarga and Central, you can hike the route, saving some money and enjoying great views of the Towers (if weather allows it). Although the path flanks the vehicle track for much of the way, there are few trekkers and the scenery is lovely so it is a tranquil experience.

Itinerary options: Section 0 is a great warm-up hike for trekkers arriving in TDPNP later in the day and starting a trek from Central the following day. However, fit hikers arriving on an early bus could tag this hike onto the first day of the W/O: O hikers could walk LA-Central-Serón on the first day; W hikers could walk LA-Central-Chileno and spend their first night at Chileno. If you are fast and fit, you could even hike LA-Central-Chileno-Mirador TDP-Chileno-Central all on the first day, spending the first night at Central: however, take note of the trail cut-off times (see p111).

Terrain	Narrow paths which are less frequented than other paths in TDPNP: slightly overgrown in places. A few short sections along a dusty track.
Route-finding	The junction at 2 is easy to miss. Otherwise, navigation is straightforward.
Accommodation/ Camping	**Laguna Amarga:** no accommodation. **Central:** see p111.
Meals/Drinks	**Laguna Amarga:** none. **Central:** see p111.
Supplies	**Laguna Amarga:** none. **Central:** see p111.
Trail notes	Central is a fragmented and confusing place: see p111.
Points of Interest	Views of the Towers.
Transport	**Laguna Amarga:** shuttle bus to Central; bus to PN, Pudeto, the Administration Centre and Lago Grey. **Central:** shuttle bus to Laguna Amarga.

The Towers at sunrise: viewed from Central

	Start	Finish	Time	Distance	Ascent (E-W)	Descent (E-W)	Max Alt
Stage 0	Laguna Amarga	Central	1:45	5.9km 3.7miles	129m 423ft	79m 259ft	140m 459ft

Walk-in: Laguna Amarga to Central

1. See map on p73. From the park buildings at **Laguna Amarga**, head N down a vehicle track. Soon cross a bridge.
2. 0:10: Shortly after crossing a second bridge, TL onto a path (easy to miss). The path is overgrown in places.
3. 0:45: The path crosses the vehicle track. A few minutes later, when you reach the track again, the path becomes faint and continues along the right side of the track: you may find it easier to walk along the track itself.
4. 1:05: Cross the track again.
5. 1:25: Cross the track and pick up a path on the other side (heading W): ignore the broader path heading N. When you reach the track again, head W along it.

(1) 1:45: Reach the **Welcome Centre** at **Central (140m)**.

Walk-out: Central to Laguna Amarga

(1) See map on p72. From the **Welcome Centre**, head E along a vehicle track. Soon TL onto a path heading E.

(5) 0:20: Cross the track and pick up a path on the other side (heading E): ignore the broader path heading N.

(4) 0:40: The path crosses the vehicle track: it becomes faint and continues along the left side of the track. You may find it easier to walk along the track itself.

(3) 1:00: Cross the track again.

(2) 1:30: TR along the track. Then cross a bridge.

(1) 1:40: Shortly after crossing a second bridge, reach the buildings at **Laguna Amarga**.

Cuernos-Central Direct Route

It is possible to hike directly between Refugio Cuernos and Central (without climbing to Chileno). This route is useful for W-E travellers who are spending the night at Central (instead of Chileno): see p110. E-W travellers can also use the short-cut if they hiked Mirador TDP the previous day and then spent the night at Central. The route passes underneath Monte Almirante Nieto and the scenery is spectacular. Laguna Inge is a wonderful place, especially if there is no wind and the nearby peaks are reflected in the water.

Terrain	The path is largely clear and well graded. However, there are a few rocky sections too.
Route-finding	Straightforward.
Accommodation/ Camping	**W end:** Cuernos (operated by Las Torres); see p103. **E end:** Central (operated by Las Torres); see p111.
Meals/drinks	**Cuernos:** see p103. **Central:** see p111.
Supplies	**Cuernos:** see p103. **Central:** see p111.
Points of Interest	Lago Nordenskjöld. Laguna Inge. Monte Almirante Nieto. Views of the Cuernos, Punta Bariloche and Cima Central.
Transport	**Central:** shuttle bus to Laguna Amarga.

	Start	Finish	Time	Distance	Ascent (ACW)	Descent (ACW)	Max Alt
Cuernos-Central Direct Route	Cuernos	Central	3:50 3:40	12.4km 7.7miles	374m 1227ft	319m 1047ft	259m 850ft

Monte Almirante Nieto and Hotel Las Torres

Cuernos-Central Direct Route

42 See map on p106. From **Refugio Cuernos**, follow Stage 7b's W-E directions to the junction at 45 (p105).

45 2:30: TR at a junction.

7 2:35: See map on p109. Shortly afterwards, cross a stream on rocks. 10min later, pass **Laguna Inge**.

6 3:00: Pass a waterfall (views restricted by undergrowth). Shortly afterwards, cross a bridge.

52 3:20: TR at a junction. Follow Stage 8b's W-E directions (p114).

1 3:50: Reach the **Welcome Centre** at **Central (140m)**.

Central-Cuernos Direct Route

1 See map on p109. Follow Stage 8b's E-W directions to the junction at 52 (p115).

52 0:30: From the junction, head initially S on a path ('Francés'). Soon the route bends right and heads SW beneath **Monte Almirante Nieto**.

6 0:50: Shortly after crossing a bridge, pass a waterfall (views restricted by undergrowth). 15-20min later, pass **Laguna Inge**.

7 1:20: Cross a stream on rocks.

45 1:25: See map on p107. Shortly afterwards, TL at a junction. Follow Stage 7b's E-W directions (p105).

42 3:35: Shortly after crossing a bridge, reach **Refugio/Camping Cuernos (85m)**.

The Q Extension: Paine Grande to the Administration Centre (Sendero las Carretas)

Sunrise across Lago Pehoé

This is one of our favourite hikes in TDPNP and makes a worthy extension to the O or W. Although it is a long and tiring route, the scenery is exquisite and there are few other hikers: many are deterred by the infrequency of buses from the Administration Centre (at the end of the hike). Heading S from PG, the path flanks the exposed shores of stunning Lago Pehoé and delivers incredible views of Cerro Paine Grande and the Cuernos across the startlingly bright turquoise waters of the lake. The climax of this part of the route is Mirador Pehoé which is one of the finest viewpoints in the park: pray for a clear day! From there, the path heads inland across grassy plains, moving away from the lake but soon meeting Río Grey. Eventually, you leave the river behind too, heading across flat grassy plains where you can spot herds of guanaco (which are less skittish in this quiet corner of the park).

In previous years, hikers could take a bus to the Administration Centre and use the Q Extension to hike S-N to PG (to start the W or O): in this direction, the views are superior because you face the massif. However, these days, you are only permitted to hike the Q Extension N-S (starting from PG) and this means that you can only use it to walk out (after completing the O or W). OTs wishing to hike the Q Extension will need to start/finish the O at PG; WTs will need to hike E-W, starting the W at Central and finishing at PG.

Although there is a good viewpoint over Lago del Toro, there are no facilities at the Administration Centre and it is not a place where you will want to spend much time. Accordingly, you should time your arrival to meet one of the few buses that pass the Administration Centre: see p121.

You can also hike the Q Extension as a day-walk: take an early bus from PN to Pudeto; catch the 10:30 catamaran from Pudeto to PG; hike from PG to the Administration Centre; and then catch the 18:00 bus from the Administration Centre to PN. You have to move reasonably quickly to ensure that you do not miss the bus.

	Start	Finish	Time	Distance	Ascent (N-S)	Descent (N-S)	Max Alt
The Q Extension	Paine Grande	Administration Centre	5:30	18.3km 11.4miles	224m 735ft	236m 774ft	76m 249ft

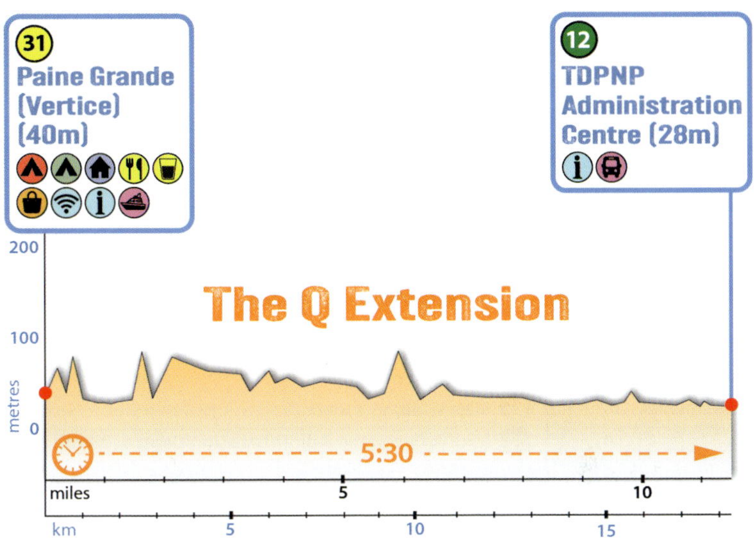

Terrain	This is a long and tiring route. At the start, there is a short, steep climb up onto cliffs: take care. Otherwise, paths/tracks are generally straightforward to negotiate (although occasionally rocky). It can be extremely windy in this part of TDPNP: in particular, take care crossing the inlet at 8 in windy conditions.
Route-finding	The route up the cliffs at the start can be tricky to follow. Otherwise, route-finding is straightforward: always remain on the main path, ignoring offshoots.
Accommodation/ Camping	**N end:** Paine Grande (operated by Vertice; see p91). **S end:** none
Meals/Drinks	**Paine Grande:** see p91.
Supplies	**Paine Grande:** see p91.
Trail notes	Allow surplus time to avoid getting stranded after the last bus has left the Administration Centre.
Points of Interest	Views of Cerro Paine Grande & the Cuernos. Grassy plains along Río Grey. Herds of guanacos.
Transport	**Paine Grande:** Lago Pehoé Catamaran between PG and Pudeto (see p45). The jetty is located 150m S of Refugio Paine Grande. Book in advance. **Administration Centre:** buses head W to HLG or E to Pudeto, LA and PN. There are two buses each day in each direction. Currently, buses heading to HLG pass at 11:00 and 16:00. Buses heading to Pudeto, LA and PN pass at 14:00 and 18:00: to catch the 14:00 bus to PN, you need to leave PG very early in the morning.

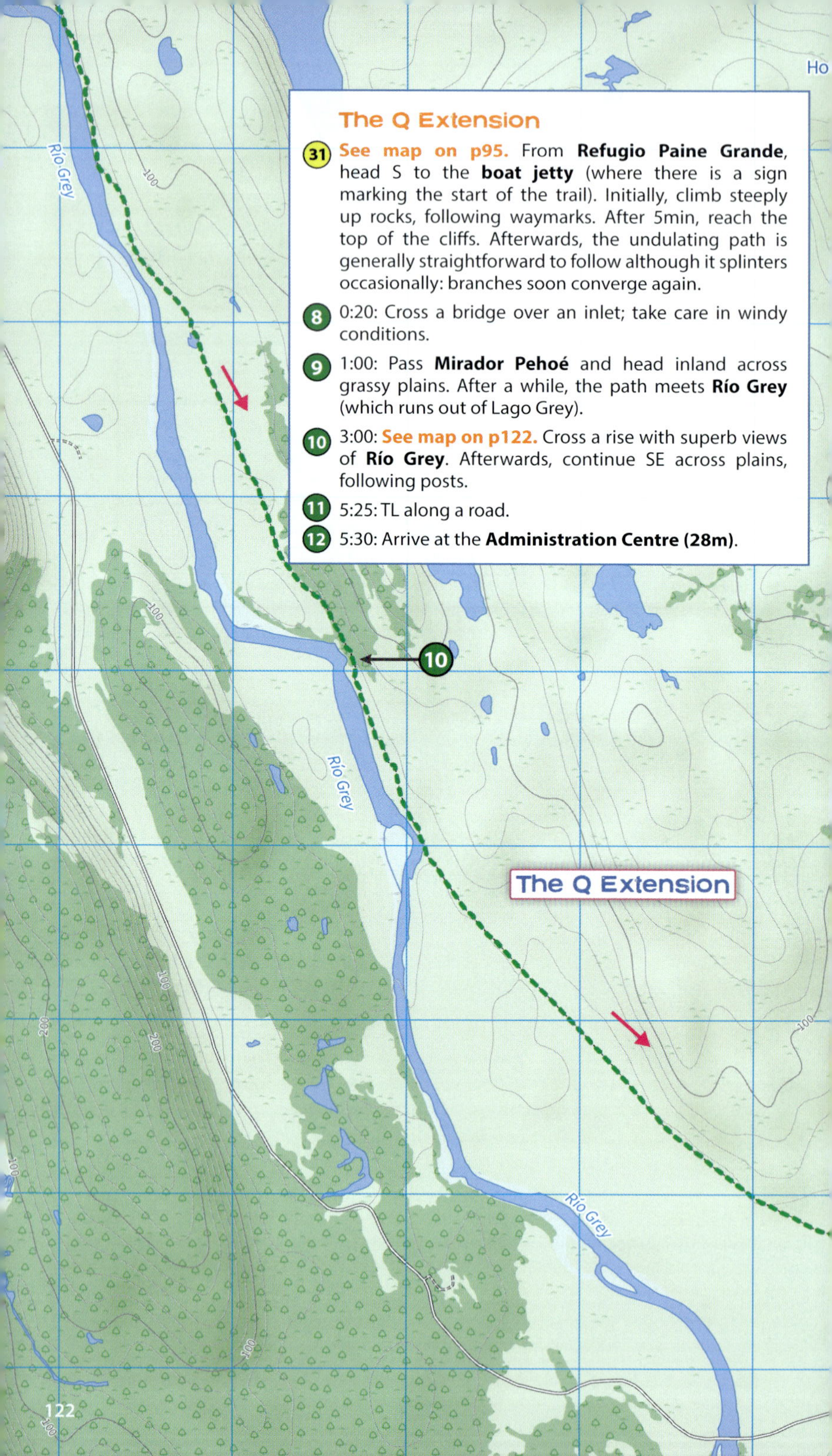
The Q Extension
31 See map on p95. From Refugio Paine Grande, head S to the boat jetty (where there is a sign marking the start of the trail). Initially, climb steeply up rocks, following waymarks. After 5min, reach the top of the cliffs. Afterwards, the undulating path is generally straightforward to follow although it splinters occasionally: branches soon converge again.
8 0:20: Cross a bridge over an inlet; take care in windy conditions.
9 1:00: Pass Mirador Pehoé and head inland across grassy plains. After a while, the path meets Río Grey (which runs out of Lago Grey).
10 3:00: See map on p122. Cross a rise with superb views of Río Grey. Afterwards, continue SE across plains, following posts.
11 5:25: TL along a road.
12 5:30: Arrive at the Administration Centre (28m).
Río Grey
Río Grey
Río Grey
10
The Q Extension
Ho
100
200

3
Pehoé(40m)
ra Patagonia
Salto Chico
Laguna Lakal
Río Paine
Laguna Los Ciervos
Laguna Linda
Mirador Torres del Paine
12
TDPNP Administration Centre (28m)
11

Day-hike 1: Salto Grande/Mirador Cuernos

The Horns viewed from the route to Mirador Cuernos

This spectacular hike visits some of the finest viewpoints in TDPNP. First up is Salto Grande, a spectacular waterfall across Río Paine (which transfers vast quantities of water from Lago Nordenskjöld to Lago Pehoé). The sight of the river's turquoise waters approaching the falls and roaring over its lip is unforgettable. The short trip to the falls alone is worth the effort and afterwards, many people simply return to the start. However, if you have time to continue to Mirador Cuernos, you will enjoy one of the finest short hikes in the world: as you head N along the shores of Lago Nordenskjöld, you are treated to sublime views of Cerro Paine Grande, the Cuernos & Glacier del Francés. Mirador Cuernos, at the N end of the trail, definitely steals the show: it looks directly across the turquoise waters of Lago Nordenskjöld onto Cerro Paine Grande and the Cuernos; if there is no wind, the reflections in the lake are stunning.

Although this hike is popular with TDPNP's day visitors, it is usually overlooked by W/O hikers (who tend to exit the park immediately after finishing their trek). Because the hike starts/finishes at Pudeto where boats to/from PG dock, it is simple to incorporate it into your W/O itinerary. For example, you can hike the route before the W/O: take an early bus from PN to Pudeto, hike to the waterfall/mirador and back, and then catch an afternoon boat to PG (where you will spend the night and start the W/O the following morning). Alternatively, you can do the hike at the end of your trek: take a morning boat from PG to Pudeto and complete the hike before taking an afternoon/evening bus back to PN that same day.

	Start	Finish	Time	Distance	Ascent	Descent	Max Alt
Salto Grande	Pudeto	Pudeto	0:50	2.8km 1.7miles	53m 174ft	53m 174ft	80m 262ft
Mirador Cuernos	Pudeto	Pudeto	2:20	7.8km 4.8miles	140m 459ft	140m 459ft	110m 361ft

Terrain	Easy, well-graded paths.
Route-finding	Straightforward.
Accommodation/ Camping	None.
Meals/Drinks	**Pudeto:** restaurant.
Supplies	None.
Trail notes	Although the terrain was devastated by a forest fire in 2011, it has now recovered well and the silvery, wizened stumps of the burnt Ñirre trees provide spectacular focal points for photographers.
Points of Interest	Salto Grande waterfall & Río Paine. Views of Cerro Paine Grande, the Cuernos & Glacier del Francés.
Transport	**Pudeto:** buses to/from HLG, the Administration Centre, LA and PN. Lago Pehoé Catamaran between PG and Pudeto (see p45).

Salto Grande/Mirador Cuernos

13 See map on p126. From the parking area at **Pudeto**, head W up a gravel road. At the end of the road, reach another parking area: take a broad path heading SW ('Salto Grande').

14 0:25: Reach a set of fabulous viewpoints overlooking **Salto Grande**. If you are not visiting Mirador Cuernos, simply retrace your steps back to Pudeto. To head to Mirador Cuernos, pick up a broad path at the upper viewpoint: head N along **Lago Nordenskjöld**; the views of the Cuernos are spectacular.

15 1:10: Arrive at **Mirador Cuernos**. After admiring the incredible panorama, retrace your steps back towards Pudeto.

13 2:20: Arrive back at **Pudeto (36m)**.

Mirador Cuernos
15
Salto Grande/
Mirador Cuernos
13
Pudeto (36m)
Salto Grande
14
Laguna Pincol
19
2
Hostería
Pehoé(40m)
18
Mirador
Condor
260
17
Mirador Condor
Mirador Cardan
16
4
Camping
Pehoé(40m)
3
Hotel Explora Patagonia
Salto Chico

Salto Grande

Day-hike 2: Mirador Condor

Mirador Condor is our favourite place in TDPNP and it is perhaps the finest place of all from which to view the entire TDP massif. It is located on an outlying hill-top which is relatively small by the standards of TDPNP, however, the views from it are anything but. Because it is set back from the principal peaks, it is a superlative vantage point from which to obtain an overall perspective of the massif: the Horns, Cerro Paine Grande and many other peaks are on full display; you can even spot Torre Sur (poking out from behind Monte Almirante Nieto). On a clear day, you will want to spend some time on the summit to identify all the peaks of the range. As a bonus, condors nest close to the viewpoint and it is common to spot them. This hike is not easily forgotten.

You can start the hike from either Hostería Pehoé or Camping Pehoé. Unless you have your own car, you will have to rely upon buses to reach these trail-heads. Although buses stop at both places, there are only two or three each day in either direction. This means that you may have time to kill after finishing the hike (which only takes about 1hr): fortunately, there are restaurants at both Hostería Pehoé and Camping Pehoé where you can get a meal while you wait. Alternatively, if you do not want to wait for the bus, you can walk along the quiet road between Pudeto and Hostería Pehoé (5.6km each way): the scenery is wonderful.

The best way to incorporate this hike into your W/O itinerary is to plan to start the W/O at PG (using the boat from Pudeto to get there) and hike Mirador Condor before starting the main trek: take a morning bus from PN to Hostería Pehoé/Camping Pehoé, hike Mirador Condor, take the afternoon bus to Pudeto and then catch the late boat to PG (where you will spend the night before starting the W/O the following morning).

You can also hike Mirador Condor after the W/O: take the 9am boat from PG to Pudeto (runs in peak season only), change onto the 10am bus from Pudeto to Hostería Pehoé/Camping Pehoé, hike the mirador and then catch an afternoon/evening bus from Hostería Pehoé/Camping Pehoé to PN. If you prefer to take a later boat from PG, you could hike Mirador Condor in the afternoon and then spend the night at Hostería Pehoé/Camping Pehoé.

	Start	Finish	Time	Distance	Ascent	Descent	Max Alt
Mirador Condor	Camping Pehoé or Hostería Pehoé	Camping Pehoé or Hostería Pehoé	1:00	2.6km 1.6miles	220m 722ft	220m 722ft	260m 853ft

Sunrise at Mirador Condor

Terrain	Mostly well-graded paths with some steep sections (particularly towards the top).
Route-finding	Straightforward.
Accommodation/ Camping	**Hostería Pehoé:** private rooms. **Camping Pehoé:** bare tent pitches; insulated domes (equipped with sleeping bags).
Meals/Drinks	**Hostería Pehoé:** restaurant. **Camping Pehoé:** restaurant
Supplies	None.
Trail notes	We provide two options for this hike: a return trip from Hostería Pehoé and a return trip from Camping Pehoé. However, it is also possible to start at one trail-head and finish at the other. Allow surplus time to avoid getting stranded in the park after the last bus has departed.
Points of Interest	Staggering views of the entire TDP massif. Condors. Incredible sunrises and sunsets.
Transport	Buses stop (on request) at both trail-heads (Hostería Pehoé and Camping Pehoé): they travel to/from HLG, the Administration Centre, Pudeto, LA and PN.

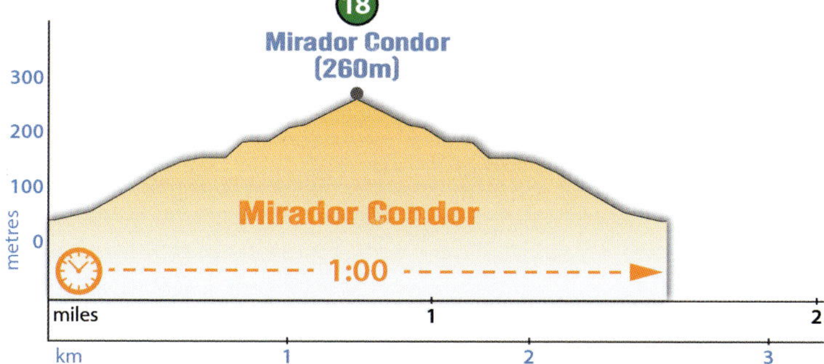

Mirador Condor (from Hostería Pehoé)

19 **See map on p126.** The route starts from a parking area which is 200m S of **Hostería Pehoé**: from there, climb gently S. Soon the path bends left and climbs more steeply.

18 0:35: TR at a junction and climb steeply W up a hill. Shortly afterwards, arrive at **Mirador Condor (260m)**. After admiring the sublime views, re-trace your steps by descending steeply E. Shortly afterwards, TL at the junction and descend N.

19 1:00: Arrive back at the **parking area** (200m S of Hostería Pehoé).

Mirador Condor (from Camping Pehoé)

16 See map on p126. The route starts from a lay-by along the road which is 100m N of **Camping Pehoé**: from there, climb E on a steep path (waymarks).

17 0:30: After a long climb, head E through a gap between two hills: Mirador Condor is on top of the hill to the left. Afterwards, the path bends left and heads briefly N around the back of the hill. Shortly afterwards, TL at a junction and climb steeply W up the hill.

18 0:35: Arrive at **Mirador Condor (260m)**. After admiring the sublime views, re-trace your steps by descending steeply E. Shortly afterwards, TR at the junction.

17 0:40: Shortly after that, TR and head W through the gap in the hills. Follow the path steeply downhill to the W.

16 1:00: Arrive back at the road (100m N of **Camping Pehoé**).

The Cuernos and Monte Almirante Nieto viewed from Hostería Pehoé

Day-hike 3: Mirador Ferrier

This viewpoint is possibly TDPNP's best kept secret. Because it is set back from the principal peaks, it is a superlative vantage point from which to obtain an overall perspective of the TDP massif. There are also fabulous views of Glacier Grey, Glacier Pingo and the park's lakes: it is fascinating to compare the grey colour of Lago Grey with the bright turquoise of Lago Pehoé. On a clear day, you will want to spend some time on the summit to identify all the peaks of the range. Look out for Huemul deer in this area.

The hike starts at Grey Ranger Station which is a short distance S of Restaurant Río Pingo. Nearby Hotel Lago Grey is the most westerly place in TDPNP that is serviced by buses: from there, it takes 10min to walk W to Restaurant Río Pingo. The best way to incorporate this day-hike into your W/O itinerary, is to finish the W/O at Refugio Grey, catch the boat from Refugio Grey to HLG the following morning, and then hike Mirador Ferrier: afterwards, you could treat yourself by spending the night at HLG and then return to PN the following day. Alternatively, catch an afternoon boat from Refugio Grey to HLG and spend the night there: the following morning, hike Mirador Ferrier and then catch a bus back to PN.

It is also possible to travel to HLG from PG. After finishing the trek, spend the night at PG: the following morning, catch the 9am boat from PG to Pudeto (peak season only), take the 10am bus from Pudeto to HLG, hike the mirador and then catch an afternoon/evening bus from HLG out of the park. If you prefer to take a later boat from PG, you could spend that night at HLG and hike Mirador Ferrier the following morning (before taking a bus back to PN).

You can also hike Mirador Ferrier before starting the W/O: take an afternoon bus from PN to HLG and spend that night at HLG: the following morning, hike Mirador Ferrier, and catch an afternoon boat to Refugio Grey (where you will start the W/O the next day). Alternatively, take a morning bus from PN to HLG, hike Mirador Ferrier, spend the night at HLG and then get the boat to Refugio Grey the following morning.

	Start	Finish	Time	Distance	Ascent	Descent	Max Alt
Mirador Ferrier	Rio Pingo Restaurant	Rio Pingo Restaurant	2:50	5.8km 3.6miles	595m 1952ft	595m 1952ft	653m 2142ft

View from near Mirador Ferrier

Terrain	A high altitude hike which should be avoided in bad weather: it can be extremely windy at the top. The forest paths are steep and muddy: slippery rocks/roots.
Route-finding	Straightforward. There is only one path and no offshoots: simply follow it to the top.
Accommodation/ Camping	**Hotel Lago Grey:** private rooms.
Meals/Drinks	**Restaurant Río Pingo** **Hotel Lago Grey:** bar/restaurant.
Supplies	**Restaurant Río Pingo:** well-stocked mini-market.
Trail notes	Before starting the hike, register at Grey Ranger Station. You can combine this route with the hike to Isla de los Hielos (p134) because they both start from the same place.
Points of Interest	Incredible views of the entire TDP massif. Lago Grey and Grey Glacier.
Transport	Buses between HLG and the Administration Centre, Pudeto, LA and PN. Boat between Refugio Grey and HLG (see p45).

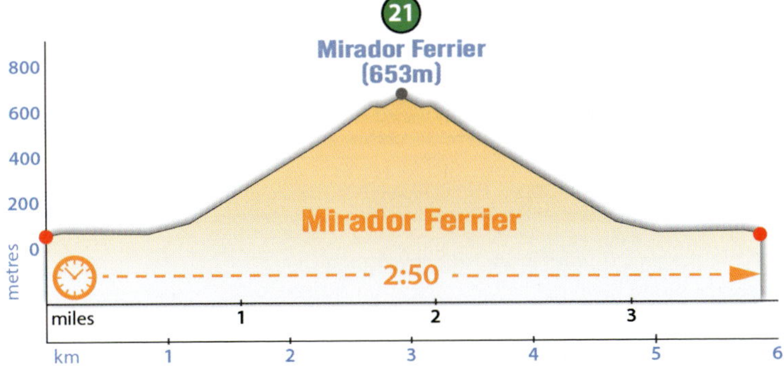

Mirador Ferrier

20 **See map on p94.** From the E side of **Grey Ranger Station**, the path heads W, winding through grassland and forest: initially, the gradient is mild. Soon, however, the path starts to climb steeply and it barely relents until the top.

21 1:40: Arrive at **Mirador Ferrier (653m)**. After admiring the views, retrace your steps back down the slope.

20 2:50: Arrive back at **Grey Ranger Station**.

Day-hike 4: Isla de los Hielos/Lago Grey Jetty

The Horns viewed from Grey Beach

This easy walk has a lot to offer. Its main destination is the beautiful Isla de los Hielos (Ice Island) which is more like a promontory than an island: the main viewpoint on its NW tip is fabulous, looking N up Lago Grey and NE onto the Horns (which light up beautifully at sunset). On the way to the promontory, you cross the black sands of the windswept Grey Beach which is the final resting place for huge icebergs which break off Glacier Grey (at the far end of the lake): in 2024, the magnificent blue iceberg which ran aground on the beach in 2017 was still there. The route also allows you to experience a beautiful section of Ñirre forest.

This hike passes Hotel Lago Grey's jetty (22) where the boat to/from Refugio Grey docks: the only way to reach the jetty is to walk between (20) and (22). This means that it is easy to combine this hike with a trip on the Lago Grey boat.

Terrain	The route across Grey Beach is quite hard work because it can be extremely windy. The path around Isla de los Hielos is slightly overgrown in places.
Route-finding	Straightforward: red posts.
Accommodation/ Camping	**Hotel Lago Grey:** private rooms.
Meals/Drinks	**Restaurant Río Pingo**. **Hotel Lago Grey:** bar/restaurant.
Supplies	**Restaurant Río Pingo:** well-stocked mini-market.
Trail notes	For information on how to incorporate this hike into your W/O itinerary, see p132: because this route starts at the same place as the hike to Mirador Ferrier, you can walk the former instead of the latter or you can combine the two hikes.
Points of Interest	Incredible views of Lago Grey and the Horns. Grey Beach and icebergs.
Transport	Buses between HLG and the Administration Centre, Pudeto, LA and PN. Boat between Refugio Grey and HLG (see p45).

	Start	Finish	Time	Distance	Ascent	Descent	Max Alt
Isla de los Hielos	Rio Pingo Restaurant	Rio Pingo Restaurant	1:45	5.6km 3.5miles	98m 322ft	98m 322ft	87m 285ft

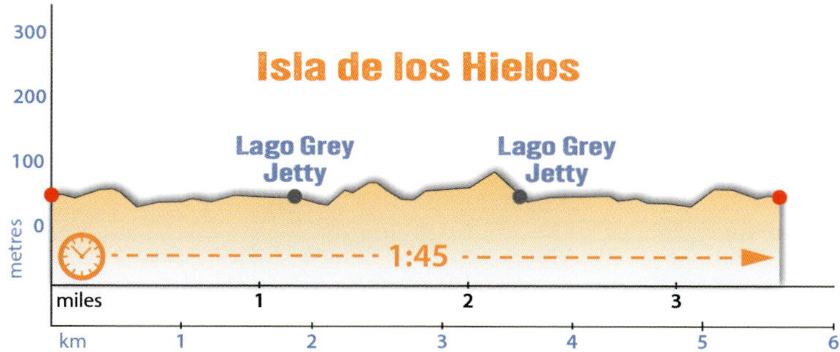

Isla de los Hielos

20 **See map on p94.** From **Restaurant Río Pingo**, head N. Soon cross a bridge over **Río Pingo**. Afterwards, head N through **Ñirre forest**. 10min from the start, emerge from the trees: bear right and walk NE along the black sands of **Grey Beach**.

22 0:35: At the E side of the beach, TL and head N along the W shore of **Isla de los Hielos**. Alternatively, TR for the **boat jetty** (which is a short distance to the S).

23 0:50: Reach a fabulous viewpoint overlooking Lago Grey and Glacier Grey. From there, a path heads CW around the promontory (red posts).

22 1:10: When the path reaches **Grey Beach** again (just N of the jetty), head W and retrace your steps back to the start.

20 1:45: Arrive back at **Restaurant Río Pingo**.

Iceberg off Grey Beach

Cerro Paine Grande

We thought hiking guidebooks were boring so we decided to change them. Mapping is better than it used to be. Graphics are better than they used to be. Photography is better than it used to be. So why have hiking guidebooks remained the same?

Well our guidebooks are **different**:

- **We use Real Maps.** You know, the **large** scale maps that walkers actually use to navigate with. Not sketch maps that get you lost. Real maps make more work for us but we think it is worth it. You do not need to carry separate maps and you are less likely to get lost so we save you time!
- **Numbered waypoints** on our Real Maps link to the walk descriptions, making routes easier to follow than traditional text-based guidebooks. No more wading through pages of boring words to find out where you are! You want to look at incredible scenery and not have your face stuck in a book all day. Right?
- **Colour, colour, colour.** Mountains and cliffs are **beautiful** so guidebooks should be too. We were fed up using guidebooks which were ugly and boring. When planning, we want to be **dazzled** with full-size colour pictures of the **magnificence** which awaits us! So our guidebooks fill every inch of the page with beauty: big, **spectacular** photos of mountains, etc.
- **More practical size.** Long enough to have useful maps and large pictures but slim enough to fit in a pocket.

Now all that sounds great to us but we want to know if you like what we have done. So hit us with your feedback: good or bad. We are not too proud to change.

Follow us for trekking advice, book updates, discount coupons, articles and other interesting hiking stuff.

www.knifeedgeoutdoor.com

info@knifeedgeoutdoor.com

@knifeedgeoutdoor

@knifeedgeout

@knifeedgeoutdoor